Project Management 101

101 Tips for Success in Project Management

Project Management 101

101 Tips for Success in Project Management

By Lew Sauder

Project Management 101
Copyright © 2014 by Lew Sauder

Edited by Stephanie S. Diamond

Library of Congress Control Number: 2014907412

Project Management 101: 101 Tips for Success in Project Management, by Lew Sauder.

ISBN 978-0-9830266-8-6

Additional copies of this book can be ordered from the publisher, CreateSpace (www.Createspace.com), or from your favorite online bookstore.

For more information, go to www.LewSauder.com

Order Lew's other books today:

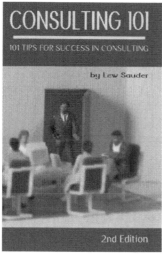

Consulting 101: 101 Tips for Success in Consulting

The Reluctant Mentor: How Baby Boomers and Millenials Can Mentor Each Other in the Modern Workplace

Dedicated to my family:
Emily, Sam, Holly, and Heather

Make no little plans; they have no magic to stir men's
blood — make big plans, aim high in hope and work.
~ Daniel H. Burnham

Acknowledgements

There have been many people throughout my life that have made this book possible.

Upon graduation from college, I began my career at a small, privately held consulting firm. Michael M. Curran was responsible for hiring me, assigning me to projects, and managing me for five years. Thank you for having confidence in me, praising me when I succeeded, correcting me when I failed, and providing a template for management and leadership that I have always tried to replicate.

During a six-year period of my career I worked with R. Gibbs Vandercook at Ernst & Young. Through that time and the many years of friendship since, I have benefitted from his project management advice as well as his leadership and support. Thank you for creating opportunities I might not have otherwise gotten, and leading me in the right direction to take advantage of those opportunities.

In the early years of my career, I worked for many project managers. I thank each of them for allowing me to learn from their successes and failures, to make me a better project manager.

Over the past four years, I have developed a professional relationship with Jeff Porter. He is my audio book voice, podcast partner, writing collaborator, and my friend. We have spent many hours, on the air and off, discussing project management, leadership principles, and success strategies. Thank you for your advice, support, creative suggestions, and friendship.

The cover art for this book was created by Jennifer Wells. Her creativity is an inspiration to me. Her work in miniature scenery photography exemplifies her talent and passion for her art. You can view Jennifer's portfolio and contact her for services at:

http://jennifernicholewells.com/.

Stephanie Diamond performed the proofreading and editing of the manuscript of this book. Her knowledge of grammar and punctuation is remarkable and her ability to wordsmith, turning content into greater meaning, never ceases to amaze me. You can contact Stephanie for her services at:

https://www.facebook.com/StephanieSmithDiamond.

Thank you to my wife, Heather Sauder, for her many years of support. Her advice and backing have created an environment that has allowed me to pursue my interests and passions throughout my career.

Thank you to my three children, Emily, Sam, and Holly. You inspire me creatively and make life interesting and fun. I hope you are as proud of me as I am of each of you.

Table of Contents

Project Management 101

Preface

What Is Project Management?

I once worked as a consultant managing a software development project that was deep into the development phase. One morning one of the team leads turned to me and asked, "What does a project manager actually do?"

As soon as he said it, he realized that it came off in a way that indicated he didn't think I did very much. He clarified in an apologetic way and I explained to him that the responsibilities change day-to-day depending on the project phase. I did my best to explain some of the responsibilities of a project manager to him.

After the conversation I started thinking that a project manager's responsibilities can seem rather ambiguous to some.

Aside from bothering the team members for their latest status – and reminding them that they are behind – people don't see a lot of the behind-the-scenes work that a project manager does. Additionally, should someone aspire to be a project manager, he may not understand all there is to do.

I decided to write this book so that those who would like to become a project manager, or who are already project managers, have a better understanding of the role.

A project, defined by the Project Management Institute (PMI), is a temporary endeavor – rather than an ongoing management task – with a defined beginning and end in order to meet an objective.

11

Project Management 101

This definition may surprise some people who have served on projects, because there is often confusion regarding a project's end and even the project's objective. Many projects meander for years only to be cancelled after wasting millions of dollars. Project management is the glue that holds a project together. Many things happen outside of the project manager's power. But with the right controls in place, a project manager can maintain order, and sometimes actually bring the project to a close.

Project management is a critical role in nearly every organization. Knowing the right things to do and the right times to do them are critical skills for a project manager.

This book is not meant to be a "how to" book on project management. Instead, it provides tips on project management intended to make a new – or experienced – project manager better. There are one hundred one tips in this book. I hope you find them helpful.

Introduction – The Merger

Holly Hewitt stared into space as she drove to work. The radio was on, but she didn't hear it. When she arrived at the high-rise office building in the Chicago suburb, she didn't remember the commute. Was there traffic? She had no idea.

She turned off the engine and sat in her seat. Her mind was racing like the wind in all directions. She trudged into the office building not even noticing the blue umbrella sky of early September.

The merger had been announced yesterday afternoon. Soon after the announcement, her boss, Alex Price, asked her to meet him in his office at nine o'clock the next morning. I guess I'm going to learn what it's like to be fired, she thought.

It wasn't as though she didn't think she could find another job. She received calls from recruiters on a fairly regular basis. It was just that she liked her job and wasn't keen on leaving.

Holly started working for Harrison Food Services when she graduated from college seven years previously. She graduated with a degree in information technology and started working as a software developer. The leadership at Harrison identified her as management material almost immediately. She wasn't just a techie. She had excellent communication skills. She worked well with the technical folks and could communicate with the business people. It wasn't long before they promoted her to team lead in charge of several developers. A few years later, they began putting her in charge of her own projects. As project manager, she managed several small- to medium-sized projects.

Harrison Food Services was a national distributor of food products including prepared soups, dairy products, and soft drinks. They were one of many companies that had courted Holly during her senior year in college. Harrison didn't offer Holly the highest salary, but they did impress her. They distributed many of the products that she used on a daily basis. But it was the people who sold her on the company. They seemed friendly but professional. It felt like the best fit for her.

And for the last seven years, it was a great fit. She made some great friends there. That, she thought, would be the most difficult thing, leaving her friends. She didn't know how many people would lose their jobs that day, but they would all start going their separate ways. She knew they would keep in touch for a while. Then they would gradually get busy with their new jobs and their new lives. It just wouldn't be the same.

All of the employees were brought into the company auditorium late yesterday afternoon to announce that they would be merging with one of their biggest competitors, Lee Food Products. Lee was another food distribution company that provided dairy products as well as a full line of prepared ready-to-eat meals to the retail grocery sector.

The presidents of each company had just finished holding a joint press conference to announce the merger which, assuming Federal Trade Commission approval, would be finalized on July first of the following year. The newly formed company would operate under the moniker of Harrison-Lee Systems.

The announcement was as unexpected and sudden as an electric shock. Everyone walked out of the auditorium stunned. The president stated that no layoffs were planned as a result of the merger, but nobody believed that. Everyone assumed there would be some cutbacks. When Holly got back to her office, she saw the e-mail from Alex asking her to meet in his office the next day. That e-mail went through her with the force of a waterfall. She felt her heart in her throat. She began to shake uncontrollably. I can't believe this is happening, she thought.

The rest of the day was a blur. She had the presence of mind to back up her personal files from her laptop. She didn't remember driving home or if she ate anything that night. She stood at her window overlooking the park until the sun descended in the west. When she went to bed, she couldn't seem to stop her racing mind. When was the last time she had updated her résumé? Who in her network should she contact first? It was all so overwhelming.

Holly sat outside of Alex's office the next morning at eight fifty-nine. His administrative assistant stuck her head in his office and asked, "Are you ready for Holly?" There was no emotion in her voice to give Holly an indication of her fate.

She heard Alex's gentle voice from inside the office. "Yes. Send her in please."

She walked in and saw her boss sitting behind his desk. His credenza was filled with various mementos, primarily from his days of playing college football. Alex was a tall, handsome man who continued to keep in shape, despite being at least ten years past his playing days. He always had a fairly serious look on his face and today wasn't an exception.

There was another man sitting in one of the two chairs across from Alex's desk. There are always two people present when they fire you, she remembered.

"Have a seat, Holly. Thanks for meeting with me this morning," Alex said.

"Sure," Holly responded. Was there a choice, she wondered.

"This is Sam Welch. He's the CIO of Lee Food Products."

"Hello, Holly," Sam said as he stood up to shake her hand.

"Good morning," she replied. At least I'm getting fired by royalty, she thought.

"There's been a lot of activity over the past few weeks as we planned yesterday's announcement of the merger," Alex continued. "We wanted to meet with you right away to tell you that I'm not going to be your manager anymore."

That's kind of a weird way to tell someone they're fired, she thought. "Oh?" was all she could force out of her shaky voice.

"Holly, I'm being reassigned to an operations role. Sam is going to be the CIO of the newly combined company. He'll be your new boss."

It took a second or two for it to sink in with Holly. Then she suddenly blurted out, "My new boss?" She took a closer look at Sam. He appeared to be around fifty. He had a round, friendly face with dark rimmed glasses that framed his smiling eyes.

"Yes," said Sam. "I've heard some great things about you, Holly. And not just from Alex. Every person I've talked to from Harrison Foods says that you're the best project manager on staff."

Holly sat there in shock. She went from expecting to get fired to being complimented by her new boss. "Thank you," she managed to squeak out as she processed the change in course her fate had just taken.

"Holly we're going to have a number of challenges as we bring together our two companies," Sam continued, "not the least of which is merging the software applications of our organizations. The reason Alex and I wanted to talk to you this morning was because we want to know if you'd be interested in heading up that project."

Holly didn't know what to say. She was still getting used to the idea of keeping her job. Now she was being offered the biggest opportunity of her career. "That sounds great," she finally said as she tried to hide the astonishment on her face.

"We're calling the project Merge-Tech," Sam went on. "It will require extensive analysis of both systems to understand how each system works and determine the best solution for combining the two systems. In addition to that, we will need you to establish and manage a team of people from both organizations, people from each company's software vendors, and third party consultants."

Holly stared at Sam incredulously. Finally Alex leaned back in his chair and said, "Well, Holly, what do you think?"

Chapter 1 – Getting Started

Holly's eyes darted between Alex and Sam. Then a broad smile appeared on her face. "This sounds like an excellent opportunity. I can't wait to get started."

"That's great, Holly," said Sam. "I know you're going to do a great job."

"Thank you, Sam," said Holly. All of a sudden, the fear of losing her job seemed a distant memory. She immediately started forging ahead. "I have a couple of initial questions. If I understand you correctly, the goal of the project is to consolidate the information technology applications for both organizations into a single system. Something I'd like to know is what drove the two companies to merge in the first place?"

"There were many things that led us to merge," Sam responded. "But there were two driving reasons. First, we were facing high distribution costs as separate firms. Both companies had their own line of trucks and delivery drivers going to virtually all of the same retail stores. By merging, we can realize some economies of scale by removing a lot of redundant distribution efforts. The second reason was information technology. Both companies have been spending above the industry average on IT. This project itself is a big part of that strategic move. We want a single modern system in place to help us run the combined company."

"That's good to know," Holly replied. "I want to make sure that the project's goals are aligned with the new organization's strategy. That's information I'll include in the project charter."

Sam smiled and nodded in agreement. They made arrangements to meet the next day to begin discussing staffing for the project. Holly walked out of Alex's office with the strangest feeling of exhilaration. What had started out as the worst day of her career had quickly pivoted to being one of the best.

Holly was eager to get started on the project. She began thinking right away about forming a team. She realized that she would need team members from both companies to ensure that there was a broad representation of knowledge of both companies' systems. She spent the rest of the day reviewing the résumés of potential team members.

The next morning she found herself sitting across from Sam's desk. Her agenda was to review the draft of the project charter she had written and begin assembling a team for the Merge-Tech project.

Sam had been with Lee Food Products for sixteen years. He started out as a project manager and served as Director of Application Development for four years before spending the last nine as the CIO.

"I read your draft of the project charter," Sam told Holly. "It looks good. The only comments I have are on the assumptions section. "

Holly raised her eyebrows. "I'm actually surprised with that. I probably spent more time on the assumptions section than any other," she said.

"I'm not surprised to hear that. You listed thirteen assumptions."

"Were there not enough?" she asked.

"No," Sam responded. "Quite the opposite. I actually thought you went a little overboard with the assumptions.

I've always felt that when you list too many, that you're doing a little too much CYA."

"CYA?"

"Cover your ass. Trying to address too many situations that you won't be responsible for. This immediately starts the project out with a feeling of distrust between the business and the project manager," said Sam.

"I hadn't thought of it that way," replied Holly.

"Don't get me wrong," said Sam. "The assumptions section is one of the most essential sections in the project charter. But it's better to document five to six overarching assumptions that explain to the business and any other interested stakeholders, the assumptions you'll be following to define responsibility, scope, and any other major issues that could come into question. It helps to get everyone on the same page. Some project managers use it as a defensive tool to inform the business community of all things they won't let the business get away with. That just sets a negative tone and starts a project off with immediate distrust at the outset."

"I see what you mean," said Holly. "I'll pare the list down a bit and make sure I list the most legitimate ones."

"Thank you. Other than that, the document looks terrific. Nice job."

Sam's knowledge of Lee's applications systems was obvious to Holly within the first ten minutes of their conversation. He began explaining the virtues of their software applications immediately and it was clear to her that he was lobbying for her to use the Lee Foods system as the basis of the functionality for the merged system.

Holly allowed him to talk, but she was more interested in focusing on staffing and determining the right team members to recruit for this critical project. She was eventually able to redirect him to that topic of conversation.

The list of people Sam proposed was a little disappointing. As Holly read through the names, she realized that Sam had followed a common selection approach that she had seen before: availability is a skill set. Anyone who wasn't already assigned to a project was put on the list. After that, she saw that most of the candidates, at least the ones he suggested for critical positions, were from Lee. He hadn't given the Harrison candidates much consideration at all.

"How did you come up with the names on this list?" she asked.

"These are the folks that are available. I put the ones I saw as better performers on top to help out a little," Sam replied.

"Looking at the résumés for each individual, some of them don't have experience in some of the technologies that we'll be working with."

Sam smiled. "Well we're going to be working with technologies that are new to many of these people. If we limit the team based on their experience with the technologies we'll be using, it will be a pretty thin team."

Holly smiled a bit defiantly. "Understood," she said, "but we need to match the team members' knowledge as closely as possible. I also want people with the right attitudes who will work well together. It's not just about technical skills and availability. If I have the right people on the team, I can train them on the technical aspects."

"So who to you suggest for the team?" Sam asked.

Holly scrutinized the list of people and lobbied for each person she wanted on the team. She had selected an architect, several developers, and business analysts. For each individual, she had an argument for why she wanted that person on the team. All of them had the right attitude. Some were known for their work ethic or for mentoring less-experienced team members.

At the end of the meeting, Holly and Sam had nailed down a team of individuals that knew the applications well enough to make the project successful.

Holly summarized the list with Sam. Kyle would be the architect with Paul as his technical lead. Together they would manage the development team. The development team would consist of Grant and Brandon, who came from Lee Foods, along with Brett and Eric from Harrison Foods.

She wanted Emily to be the lead business analyst. Holly had worked with her before at Harrison Foods and had been impressed with her attention to detail and probing questions. Sam acquiesced to her proposal. Emily would oversee the work of Chris and John, two business analysts from Lee Foods.

Finally, Sam and Holly agreed that Danielle would be the database analyst. She would oversee Dominic, an experienced database developer.

"You've obviously done your homework on each of these people," Sam said. "You've also picked a team with good representation from both companies. I think that shows that you didn't use favoritism in your selection. I'm comfortable going with your list. You can begin contacting them as soon as you're ready."

Holly left the meeting satisfied that she had selected the right people for the project to be successful. Some of the team members would require some training. But she had confidence that she had the right staff to succeed.

She knew she would still have a lot of decisions to make on how to approach the project, but she felt she had the right players in place in order to make those decisions.

Lessons Learned

Tip #1 – Know how the project supports the strategy of the organization

One of the first documents a project manager creates is the project charter. The project charter should define the high-level scope and objectives of the project as well as the project purpose – how it fits into the strategy of the organization.

The project charter is the driver behind most project decisions. It is usually a short reference document but it can be used throughout the project for new team members coming on board, or to remind any stakeholder of the project purpose.

Tip #2 – Document legitimate assumptions

There is often a tendency by project managers to cover as many assumptions in the project charter as they can come up with. The purpose of assumptions in the charter is to clarify what will and will not be part of the project. Providing too many assumptions gives the appearance of being defensive and may cause the business users to raise their guard, creating a first impression of distrust.

Tip #3 – Staff the right people

Another critical responsibility of the project manager in the initial stages of a project is identifying the right people for each role. While many managers simply choose the most available people, this can result in putting square pegs in round holes.

Project Management 101

Jim Collins calls it, "Getting the right people on the bus," in his book *Good to Great*[1]. It is critical to make sure you match the right skills and attitudes for success, even if you have to swap people out of another project or go outside of the company.

[1]Collins, Jim, *Good to Great: Why Some Companies Make the Leap…And Others Don't.* New York: HarperBusiness, 2001.

Chapter 2 – Preparation, Planning, and Pete

A bird sat on the windowsill of Holly's office, distracting her momentarily from her work. A knock on the door startled her. She turned around to see a tall, thin man about her age. He had horn-rimmed glasses and a shirt with a frayed collar.

"Hi, I'm Pete," he said with a smug grin and an outstretched hand.

"Hi Pete, I'm Holly Hewitt," she said, reaching out to shake his hand.

Pet sat down without invitation. Perhaps he assumed Holly had time to talk since she was staring out the window, but he didn't bother to ask. "So you're managing the Merge-Tech project," he said.

She wasn't sure if it was a statement or a question. "Yeah, that's what they tell me."

Pete crossed his legs and locked his fingers behind his head. "I've been a project manager with Lee Foods for a couple of years now. Sam probably would have picked me to manage this one, but I'm swamped with too many other projects right now."

"Is that right?" In the few moments that Holly had known Pete, she sensed something she didn't like. She couldn't put her finger on it. He just didn't seem likable.

"Yeah, I'm kind of Sam's right-hand man," he boasted. "He has me manage a lot of his projects. How long were you with Harrison?"

"About seven years," she answered.

"Cool. So are you in the requirements gathering phase now or are you still in start-up?"

"We're still in start-up mode. I've been trying to decide whether to use an agile approach where we can break down the functionality into multiple iterations or if we want the more traditional waterfall approach of getting all the requirements up front and developing it all together. I'm actually leaning toward a hybrid of the two."

"Don't use agile!" Pete demanded. "It's a fad. The traditional approach is really the only way to go with a big project like this."

"Oh, have you used agile before?" Holly asked impassively.

"No," answered Pete. "I've read a lot about it and talked to people who have used it. Believe me, you don't want to get into that here. I'll send you some of the templates I've used on my projects. That should get you started," he said as he got up to leave. "I sit upstairs by the break room if you ever have any questions. Maybe we could do lunch sometime."

"Thanks, maybe," Holly responded without commitment.

A quiet fury rose within her for few minutes after Pete left. He dropped by under the pretense of offering help, she thought. But she sensed an ulterior motive. She vowed to keep her guard up around him.

She glanced at the clock and realized how late it was. Her mother was having a get-together that night and she didn't want to be late.

Holly pulled up in front of her mother's condo and turned off the engine. She had been looking forward to this party. It had been an eventful week and she was ready to relax and have a little fun.

Ann Hewitt was not only Holly's mother, she was her best friend. Ann was director of operations at Stewart Bicycle, a local bicycle manufacturing company. Holly enjoyed cycling and enjoyed her mother's discount on equipment.

Holly had always looked up to her mom. She was the smartest person Holly knew. Ann had a certain aptitude for understanding an issue and asking the right questions to lead Holly to the right answer rather than just telling her what to do.

Ann greeted Holly with a big hug when she walked in. There was already about a half dozen people there. Ann led Holly to the kitchen and introduced her to Raul. Ann had met Raul at a networking event and thought he and Holly would have a lot in common since he worked in information technology, too. Ann was secretly hoping that a more serious relationship would result, but she didn't dare mention that to Holly.

"Nice to meet you," they both said in near unison.

"Ann mentioned that you're a project manager," said Raul. "What methodology do you follow?"

"I'm considering following a bit of hybrid approach of agile and waterfall. I wouldn't say it's a formal methodology," Holly said.

"That's kind of scary," replied Raul, waving his hand in a gesture of contempt.

"Why do you say that?" Holly asked, a little taken aback.

"I just think it's important to follow a formal methodology for project management."

"What methodology do you follow?" Holly asked, taking his bait.

Project Management 101

"I work for Central Hub Consulting. You've probably heard of our CHUM methodology. It stands for Central Hub Unity Method."

Raul talked much longer than it took for Holly to dislike him. He rambled on about their proprietary methodology. He gave her his business card and explained why her company should hire his firm to manage their project.

What a great idea, she thought. Why didn't I think of replacing myself with a pompous ass like you?

When he finally stopped to take a breath, Holly considered him for a moment and asked, "What is unique about CHUM that ensures project success?"

"Well, it's too complex to describe in detail here, but it consists of five defined phases with all of the processes within them defining what needs to be done in each one. It ensures that everything is done right at the right time."

Holly held the stem of her wine glass, whirling it slowly between two fingers. "I've used a few methodologies in the past," she responded. "I've found them to be sort of like recipes. People tend to follow them to the letter without thinking about what they're trying to accomplish. Don't get me wrong. I think methodologies serve a purpose, as long they're used as a guideline and not a gospel."

From there, the conversation went downhill. After the week Holly had had, she wasn't in the mood to argue and she knew that any further discussion was useless. Raul wasn't able to convince her that his, or any other methodology, would ensure success and she decided it was best if they agreed to disagree. She excused herself to get another drink.

She poured herself a glass of wine and noticed her mother talking with a handsome man about Holly's age. She walked up and nudged herself into the conversation. He and her mother were discussing something about work and Holly presumed that he was one of her mother's coworkers.

Ann saw Holly standing there and drew her into the conversation. "Chad, this is my daughter, Holly. Holly this is Chad Harrison. Chad has been a consultant for us at Stewart Bicycle."

They glanced at each other and smiled. "Pleased to meet you," Holly said.

"The pleasure's mine," Chad replied.

After chatting for only a minute or two, Ann sensed something between them. She had evidently struck out with Raul but something might just be brewing with Chad. Either way, she felt like an intruder in her own home in this conversation.

"I think I'll go freshen up my drink," Ann said to the oblivious couple.

Holly and Chad hit it off immediately. They sat on the couch and talked for nearly two hours straight. Chad had managed projects before using both agile and waterfall methods. Although he preferred an agile approach, he explained the pros and cons of each without trying to sell her on either one. Although most of the evening's conversation revolved around shop talk, they both seemed to enjoy each other's company.

As the evening wound down, they noticed people starting to say their good-byes. "How about we meet for coffee sometime and discuss the project approaches in more detail?" Chad suggested.

"Oh, I don't think so," Holly replied.

Chad cocked his head with a look of disappointment on his face.

Holly smiled, "I think dinner would be a better idea."

A wide grin replaced Chad's look of disappointment. "You got it," he said.

The next Monday morning, Holly entered Sam's office for her first official one-on-one session with him. She was a bit apprehensive. She still didn't know Sam very well and he didn't know her any better. He was on the phone when he saw her in the doorway and waved her in, pointing to one of the two chairs opposite his desk. He finished the conversation quickly and hung up.

"Sorry about that, Holly," he said. "That call went longer than it needed to. How are things going?"

"Things are going fine," she replied. "I've been debating whether to use an agile approach to this project or to follow a more traditional waterfall approach. I'm leaning toward a hybrid approach that integrates the two."

"The approach you use doesn't really matter to me," Sam said. "I think a good project manager can be successful using whatever approach or methodology he or she is comfortable with. Let me ask this. Are you familiar with the three layers of management?"

Holly thought for a few seconds. "No, I can't say I am."

Sam walked up to the whiteboard on his wall and picked up a dry-erase marker. "I've always looked at project management as having three layers." He wrote down the word *Administrative*. "The lowest layer is the administrative layer. This involves paying attention to the project's basics. Some project managers call this the recording and reporting layer. In this layer, the project manager's responsibilities include gathering status updates from team members, updating your project plan, scheduling status meetings, and consolidating the status information for the next level of management. It also includes collecting hours reported by team members and tracking financials to maintain the project budget. Does this all make sense?"

Holly nodded her understanding as she scrawled in her notebook.

Next, Sam wrote *Management* on the whiteboard above the word *Administrative*. "The next layer is the management layer," he continued. "This is where a project manager attends to some of the more complex aspects of the project. At this layer, you'll assess aspects such as project risks – what could go wrong, issues – what did go wrong, scope changes, and due dates for tasks. As a project manager, you'll need to use a tool that helps you track this information that is accessible for any of the project stakeholders who need to see it. You'll also need to develop mitigation strategies to address the risks if they become actual issues and address issues promptly. Still with me?"

Holly nodded again. "This all makes sense. What's the third layer?" she asked in anticipation.

"Good," Sam said. "The third layer is where most project managers fail." He wrote *Leadership* on the whiteboard above the other two words. "The third and highest layer of project management involves being a capable leader. To be effective as a project manager, you have to stay close to your business customers, the people who will ultimately be using the product that you and your team will deliver. You need to understand their business needs, even when they don't communicate them effectively. You need to always keep in mind that the final product that your team delivers, needs to be an effective business tool rather than a list of business requirements that can be checked off by the development team.

"In addition to all of that," Sam went on, "to be a good leader you need to develop a relationship with each member of your team. You need to get to know each individual and understand how this project can help him or her accomplish his or her career goals. Once you develop a familiarization with each team member, you should adapt your leadership style to get the highest productivity from each person. For instance, for team members who work best under pressure, you may need to maintain enough pressure to keep them motivated while avoiding exerting too much pressure to the point where they get overwhelmed. At the same time, there may be team members who don't respond well to pressure. Identifying this style of team member and determining the best approach to keep them motivated and productive is critical."

Sam put the cap back on the dry-erase marker, placed the marker back in the tray, and sat down. After giving it a moment to sink in he asked, "Does all this make sense?"

Holly finished her note taking and looked up at Sam. "Yes," she said. "I know I'm good at the first two layers. And I think I'm pretty good at the leadership layer, but I know that will be the biggest challenge."

"It always is. And it's the most important. If you only focus on the first two, it's possible to succeed. But focusing on all three layers increases your chances of success not only on the project, but for your career and the careers of your teammates."

"I'll focus on all three. But I may need some direction on the leadership layer," Holly said.

"That's what I'm here for," said Sam. "I'll answer any questions you have and give advice along the way. Holly, I wouldn't have picked you to manage this project if I wasn't one hundred percent certain that you could handle all three layers."

Holly left the one-on-one session feeling challenged and a bit overwhelmed, but invigorated. This project, she thought, is a huge opportunity for me. I hope I don't blow it.

Lessons Learned

Tip #4 – Determine your own approach to managing the project

There is much debate these days regarding managing projects in an agile approach, a waterfall approach, or some combination of the two. Some people have strong opinions of the "correct" way. But there is no perfect approach. A project manager must choose the approach that works best for his or her management style and for all stakeholders involved. Once one is chosen, the project manager should make sure that the entire stakeholder community is educated on the approach so that expectations are realistic.

Tip #5 – Methodology doesn't determine success

Like the approach to project management, the methodology used does not guarantee success. Many methodologies provide step-by-step instructions and processes that try to keep the project manager from forgetting any steps. The downside is that the project manager can rely too heavily on the process. When issues occur that fall outside the parameters of the methodology, the project manager may not know how to handle the situation or it may fall through the cracks because the methodology didn't have it on the project manager's radar.

Tip #6 – Manage the project's three layers

More important than any approach or methodology, a project manager must make certain that she covers the administrative, management, and leadership aspects of the project. Leadership is the most important of these layers to insure success. It is the most complex but is the one layer that is most often neglected.

Project management is much more than asking team members for status updates and tracking issues and scope. A good project manager learns to develop relationships with each stakeholder and adjust her approach accordingly.

Chapter 3 – Kicking It off with the Team

The project team members poured into the conference room and grabbed their seats. At exactly two o'clock Holly started talking. "Thanks for coming, everyone. I hope you're all as excited about this project as I am."

She heard a few chuckles from the crowd and wasn't surprised. "I'm actually serious about that," Holly said. "As you know, this is a huge project, bigger than any project attempted by either Lee Food Products or Harrison Distribution Systems. And while I know it's going to be a lot of work, this is a huge opportunity for everyone here. If this project is successful – and I have every expectation that it will be – everyone in this room will be in the driver's seat for the next step in their career."

Walking up to an easel pad, she addressed the team. "The first thing I'd like to do is to develop some team norms. Is anyone familiar with the team norm concept?"

She saw several blank faces and a few head shakes so she continued.

"Team norms are just a few guidelines that we agree upon as a team to make sure we're all on the same page. It also makes sure everyone has a mutual respect for each other."

Grant raised his hand first, "You mean like a set of rules and regulations?"

"I prefer to think of them as customs, things we do in our normal day so that we work together better," Holly said.

"How about being on time?" Grant asked.

It was hard for Holly to hide her joy that someone else came up with it. "Does everyone like that one?" she asked.

Seeing everyone shake their heads in agreement she said, "How about if we say 'Promptness is a sign of respect'?"

Everyone agreed and she wrote it on the large pad.

"What else?" she asked.

Someone else raised his hand. "How about not eating at our desks? Sometimes it can be distracting when I'm trying to finish something and someone is eating something that smells really good. My hunger won't let me concentrate."

A few people laughed, but when Holly surveyed the room about this team norm, no one objected and she added it to the list.

"Oh, that's another thing. How about this?" She added to the list, "Silence is agreement."

"If you disagree with anything we say – in any meeting – you'd better speak up, otherwise, I'm going to assume you agree." After an appropriate moment of silence, she asked, "Any others?"

Emily suggested they schedule their daily stand-up meetings and begin polling each team member for the best available time. "We should contact the user community to determine the best times to schedule requirements gathering sessions," she added.

The team members started coming up with additional ideas. The team unanimously agreed to some. There was discussion about other ideas and they were either reworded as a team norm or voted down. By the time they were done, Holly had facilitated the team to provide all of the norms that the group wanted.

"Now," Holly said, "we will all hold each other to these team norms. We'll revisit the list each time we plan a new iteration of work. We can add, modify, or remove these rules at that time. Until then everyone is responsible to the rest of the team to uphold these norms.

Holly tore off the large sheet with the list of team norms to hang up on the team room wall. She could sense that the team was glad that they had gone through that exercise.

Holly's next agenda item for the meeting was to brainstorm for ideas on implementation options. "Each of us probably has a bias toward the system that they are most familiar with. It will be critical to keep an open mind with a goal of working toward the right solution rather than any predisposition of how anyone thinks it should be done," she explained to the team.

At that point, someone said, "This is a big project isn't it?"

Holly stopped and looked at the team. "This is more than just a big project. This project could decide the future of Harrison-Lee Systems. We have the chance to turn two good companies into a great consolidated organization. One of the driving purposes behind this corporate merger is the complementary IT assets these two companies have."

"That's good for each of us too, right?" asked Emily.

"Absolutely," Holly said. "You were selected for this project because we thought you were the best of the best. The more successful this project is, the more successful each of you will be."

Holly turned to the whiteboard and wrote, *It's amazing what we can accomplish when nobody cares who gets the credit.*

Then she turned to face the team. "Let's dedicate ourselves as a team to making this a successful project."

Everyone in the room nodded in agreement.

She paused for another moment to let the effect of the project's importance sink in with everyone. "Now," she continued, "let's talk about possible solutions."

The team members began discussing how they thought they should begin merging the software applications of the two merging firms. Emily spoke up first, "I'm most familiar with Harrison's applications, but I know that Lee's order processing module is strong. My initial thought was that we should build the system around Lee's order entry strengths and use the best applications from each company. Then maybe we would have to custom develop some applications to make sure it's a well-integrated product."

Holly stopped the conversation there. "Time out folks. We need to narrow our approaches to a few of our best ideas; maybe have one that we recommend; and then get the business team's approval.

The team brainstormed several options and pared the list down to what they saw as the four most viable options to consider.

The first option they considered was selecting Harrison's applications as the primary system and integrating any functionality that Lee had that the Harrison system lacked.

On the other hand, they could conclude that Lee's applications have more usable functionality and use it as the base system, enhancing it with complimentary functionality from Harrison's applications.

The third option was to scrap both systems and write a well-integrated system from scratch. This could eliminate extensive work weaving two disparate systems together, resulting in a large inefficient system that could be difficult and expensive to maintain.

The fourth and final option they considered was to replace both systems with a packaged application that would fit all – or most – of their needs and be written with standard industry practices, allowing them to easily interface with third-party applications.

The team agreed that they would complete a three-week discovery phase, in which they would do an in-depth analysis of each application, identify available packages that serve their industry and come up with a recommendation for an approach that best meets their newly merged organization's needs.

With the team kick-off out of the way, Holly was ready to set her sights on another group -- the business stakeholders.

Lessons Learned

Tip #7 – Hold an internal kick-off meeting

It is important to bring the implementation team together at the beginning of the project to formally kick things off. The internal kick-off meeting allows the project manager to present an overview of the project to the team, define roles and responsibilities, and set expectations for everyone up front. It is also an excellent opportunity for the team members to begin getting to know each other.

Tip #8 – Define team norms and expectations

An effective tool during an internal kick-off is to allow the team to define what it means for everyone to treat each other with respect. This allows each team member to know what is expected of them and permits any team member to call out another when one fails to comply with the team norms. Team norms should be posted prominently wherever the team works or meets regularly.

Tip #9 - Inspire a shared team vision

Everybody on the team needs to have the same vision of the purpose of the project including what it means to each of them individually. A good project manager communicates a shared vision to the team early on to ensure that each team member is working toward that goal.

Tip #10 – Consider multiple options for the project solution

There are countless ways to solve any problem. At the beginning of a project, the project manager has a blank slate regarding how to implement a solution. Holly facilitated this with the team, which came up with many possible solutions. From there, they pared the list down to a few manageable options to investigate further to determine the most effective solution for the newly merged company.

Tip #11 – Promote collaboration and decision making with the team

Instead of dictating the team norms and possible solutions to the team, Holly facilitated a conversation. She involved the team in the process, which insures buy-in and involvement from the team throughout the project. The team members are more likely to see the solution as their solution rather than the one that was imposed on them.

Chapter 4 – Addressing the Stakeholders

Holly drove to work with the sunroof open. It was a warm morning in late September and there was a first touch of cool crispness in the air. She decided to savor the few pleasant mornings remaining before the Chicago weather inevitably turned colder.

As Holly got out of her car, she recognized Emily's car pulling into the parking lot and waited for her.

"Beautiful morning, isn't it?" Holly greeted.

"It sure is. There probably aren't a lot of mornings like this left in the year," Emily returned.

Holly smiled and nodded in agreement.

As they walked into the building, their attention turned to business. "I saw your e-mail yesterday about the templates I use for requirements," Emily said. "Why do you need them?"

"I'd like to review them with the users to get their approval," Holly said. "I also want their feedback on the approval process."

Emily wasn't sure she understood, but was happy comply.

Later that morning, Holly stood alone in front of the auditorium. Scores of the company's business users gradually packed the seats in the big room.

The dull roar of the many conversations grew louder and louder. As Holly watched the clock turn to nine o'clock she spoke up.

"Let's get started," she announced. The crowd quieted down and gave Holly their attention. "We're here to talk about the project to merge the software applications of Lee Food Products and Harrison Food Services. The project has been named Merge-Tech because we will be merging the technologies of both companies. We feel that one of the things that make this merger a good idea is that each company has technology components that we can combine to make the whole greater than the sum of the parts."

Holly described the benefits that the newly merged system would bring to the new organization. She presented the project's goals and showed them the proposed schedule for the project, explaining that the planned project completion date was June thirtieth of the following year. She then went over the expectations from each stakeholder over that period of time.

After giving a high-level overview of the project, she turned on the projector, which shone on the white screen. She displayed each of the templates that Emily and other team members had provided. For each one, Holly reviewed the main sections and subsections explaining the purpose of each deliverable.

Once each document had been reviewed, Holly stopped and asked the group if they would like to modify the template in any way or if it was acceptable in its current form. Every once in a while, someone would suggest a tweak, but generally each template was approved.

When all of the document templates had been reviewed Holly asked the group, "What is the appropriate amount of time to allow you to review each of these deliverables before we can expect either feedback or an approval? My preference is two business days. Does anyone have a problem with that?"

The meeting attendees considered her suggestion. After a moment of murmuring, the group unanimously agreed to the two-day time period.

"Finally," Holly concluded, "I'd like to establish how you want to approve deliverables for this project. We used to get physical signatures on a hard copy of the document, but we do most of this electronically these days. If I send documents out via e-mail for approval, my preference is for each of you to just reply to the e-mail with the message 'Approved.' Does everyone agree with this?"

Again, the group nodded approval in unison.

With such a diverse group, including people from both companies, vendors, and consultants, Holly knew that communication would be critical. She wanted to document the standard expectations for formal communication to make sure nothing was left to chance.

In some of the projects that she had managed in the past, she simply included a communications section in the project charter. With a project this important and this large, she decided to make the communications plan a separate document.

She projected the communications plan on the wall to show everyone she had defined all the appropriate stakeholders that need to be informed of any changes in documentation. Each recurring meeting was defined with its time, place, attendees, and purpose.

For the next agenda item of the meeting, Holly displayed a slide that stated simply *What is success?* Holly gave everyone a moment to consider the question and asked, "What do we need to do by June thirtieth of next year for everyone here to consider this project a success? Please keep in mind that we need to have some portion of it in production by that date. There will be follow-on phases in which we will continue to add functionality."

Someone yelled out, "A single consolidated system."

Holly smiled and said, "That's great. Can you be more specific? What is the minimum functionality you would need to be able to say on June twenty-ninth, 'Yes, we can go live tomorrow'?"

Someone else spoke up, "The ability to run an order from the initial customer contact through the full system and get the product on the shelf."

As people shouted out suggestions, Holly began to write the various ideas down on the whiteboard.

One woman stood up and said, "I know you mean well, but I'm just very leery of these follow-on phases. I've seen projects where they are promised to get us to give in on functionality. Then when the first phase is finished, they never get around to these follow-on phases. How can I trust that we will get the functionality we need? What if these follow-on phases never happen?"

Many in the group nodded and voiced agreement.

Holly put both hands up and tried to calm the crowd down. "I can guarantee there will be at least one – and probably more – follow-on phase. There is no way we can get all of our needed functionality in by June thirtieth of next year. We will have to have a second phase. The point of the first phase is to get the mission critical items – the bare essentials – in by that date. Then we will continue to build on the system."

Holly knew she might have convinced a few of them, but not everyone. Finally she said, "We're almost out of time here, but I would like to continue this conversation. Let's do this: I'd like each of you to think about what functionality you absolutely need by June and what you can live without until a second phase is implemented. I'll work with our executives to see what I can do about having them commit to follow-on phases that will satisfy your concerns."

The group seemed open to Holly's suggestion and began filing out of the room.

The next morning, Holly met with Sam and explained the business team's concern.

"There's no way we can get all of this implemented by June," Sam said. "There has to be a second and probably a third phase of this project."

"We both know that," responded Holly, "but how do we convince them of that?"

"I'll attend your next meeting and personally guarantee it," Sam said.

"That would be great," Holly said. "What if we also took the first step in sacrificing functionality? We could list all of the functionality that the IT group is willing to do without in the June release to show that we're serious about this."

"That's a good idea," Sam said. "It will set a good example of doing without functionality for the first phase."

The following week, Holly and Sam met with the business team and showed them a list of reports and executive functionality that the technical team was willing to sacrifice in the first release. Holly saw several of last week's nonbelievers nod their heads in approval.

Throughout the rest of the hour, she was impressed with the list of functionality that the business team volunteered that they were willing to live without until a second phase.

When she closed the meeting, the business users left energized with the correct expectations for the Merge-Tech project. Holly knew there would be issues, questions, and concerns throughout the project, but she knew she had set the groundwork for understanding with her audience that would start the project off on the right foot.

Lessons Learned

Tip #12 – Kick off the project with the key business stakeholders

After kicking the project off with the internal team, another essential task for a project manager to do at the beginning of the project is to hold a kick-off meeting with the business stakeholders. This allows the project manager to start the communication process successfully. In the business stakeholder kick-off meeting, the project manager should set expectations with the business people regarding the scope and timeline of the project, define how the primary routes of communication will be handled and obtain the stakeholders input on how deliverables will be approved.

Tip #13 – Agree on deliverable acceptance criteria in advance

Throughout the project, business requirements, technical documents, and many other deliverables will be generated by the team for approval by various project stakeholders. It is critical to define the acceptance criteria for each set of documents and establish expectations with both sides for feedback. Setting these expectations at the beginning of the project eliminates confusion and frustration down the road.

Tip #14 –Obtain agreement on a communications plan

Communication is one of the most important elements of any project. It takes place in meetings, e-mails, spoken word, and any number of formal and informal avenues. Establishing a communications plan that details how the project team and stakeholders will communicate eliminates many potential issues. A critical part of the communications plan is to define when recurring meetings will be held, who is expected to attend, and the purpose for each meeting.

Tip #15 – Have an end game -- define project success

A project manager can define a project timeline, the scope, and the budget for a project. But finishing a project on time and within budget is not a guarantee for providing value to the business. The project manager should have a clear idea of what the business stakeholders consider success for the project. Defining their concept of success sets the foundation for the project manager's decision making throughout the project.

Tip #16 –Be customer focused

As soon as the business users expressed doubts about the possibility of any follow-on phases, Holly knew that she had to set their minds at ease. She resolved the issue, and in the process, developed deeper trust with the business stakeholders. If she had not resolved the issue to their satisfaction, she would most likely have had to deal with more functionality in the scope of the first phase of the project than the team could do before the deadline. Including Sam and offering to sacrifice technical functionality set an example that encouraged the business users to follow suit.

More than that, Holly showed the business users that she was focused on their concerns and showed a willingness to address those concerns without forcing her agenda on them.

Chapter 5 – Risky Business

Holly gazed out the window of the conference room as her team filed in. She watched the leaves as they blew in the early fall wind. She noticed they were beginning to turn colors. The small talk began to fade and Emily turned to Holly and asked, "So what is this risk analysis meeting all about?"

Holly saw the rest of the eyes turn to her as if Emily had taken the words out of their collective mouths.

"Exactly that," Holly said. "We're going to analyze risks. I'm generally a positive person and I try to encourage that attitude with the team. But today, I want everyone here to turn on their pessimistic attitudes. I want to discuss the risks that we face on Merge-Tech. Let's brainstorm on the things that could go wrong on the project, the things that keep us up at night."

"What's the purpose of this?" Brett asked.

Holly smiled as if she was hoping someone would ask that. "Well, if we're aware of what could go wrong, we can develop mitigation plans before it happens. I had a boss once who was a fighter pilot. He told me that whenever he went up in his plane, he had to be ready for anything--his engine could go out, he could get shot at, all kinds of things. He said he always had a mental list of things that could happen and what he'd do in each case. It sounded a little depressing to me, but that's what we need to do for Merge-Tech. That way, we'll be ready for almost anything. I'll give you an example."

She went to the whiteboard and wrote, *New database servers are delayed and don't get delivered on time*. Then she turned back to face the team. "This is one of the things that keeps me up at night. We need to order new servers. We've been working on figuring out what we need. Then we'll go through the budget approval process. I'm sure it will get approved. It's just a matter of how long it takes to get all of the signatures. Then when we submit the order, we will have no control over how long it will take. They may be able to process the order and get the equipment to us in two weeks and we'll be fine. But what if they have to order parts and it takes eight weeks? Or worse yet, what if they go out of business? We need to have a backup plan in place to be ready for these risks."

Emily raised her hand. "I worry about all of the meetings we have. Sometimes I feel like I spend the whole day in meetings and I don't have time to document the business requirements."

"That's a great one," Holly said as she added it to the list. "What other kinds of things can get in your way of getting your jobs done?" she asked the team.

The team started raising their hands and offering ideas faster than Holly could write them down, but she managed to get each one recorded. Some had remote chances of happening, but she would assess the likelihood when they went through with mitigation plans.

After about thirty minutes of brainstorming, the team had come up with several risks. A few people started packing up their notepads and laptops, believing they were finished.

Then Holly drew a line down the right side of the list. "Now comes the hard part," she said. "What do we plan to do about these risks?"

After a few sighs, everyone sat back and continued to listen.

"Identifying these risks is nice, but it's not enough," she went on. "What do we need to do to either avoid having these risks occur, prevent them from becoming actual issues, or handle the ones that may be out of our control? In those cases we may just decide to accept the risk."

"What do you mean?" Grant asked.

Holly offered a glad-you-asked-that smile to Grant and continued on. "Well, take this risk," she said, pointing to *Hardware could be delayed by the vendor*. "After we place that order, we don't have much control over it. One thing we could do is repurpose the existing hardware that we have on site. That would be risk avoidance. But we would also end up creating an all-new risk by using older equipment."

"We could have another supplier as a backup," Grant suggested. "We can option hardware with our second supplier choice at a nominal cost in case our first choice is unable to get it on time."

Holly wrote that down next to the risk. "That's preventative risk mitigation. It's sort of like taking out an insurance policy. We're willing to pay a premium and hope we don't have to use it. There's one other option. We could just accept the risk. If we think the likelihood is low that it will happen or if the delay won't affect us that much, we could just accept it and move on."

The team seemed to understand the different approaches to mitigation. Holly walked them through each of the risks on the list as they came up with as many mitigation options as they could think of for each one. By the time they were finished, they had multiple mitigation strategies for each risk on the list.

The next day Emily stopped by Holly's office to see if she was ready for lunch.

"Are you working on another spreadsheet?"

"What do you mean another one?" Holly asked defensively.

"You just always seem to be working on one spreadsheet or another."

"I don't create that many. Anyway it's a good tool for tracking things."

"What's this one for? Emily asked.

"It's for tracking all of the risks for the project."

"The risks we came up with in the meeting yesterday?"

"Those and more that I had identified with Sam and some of the executives." Holly turned her monitor around and showed Emily the spreadsheet. For each risk listed, she had assigned a likelihood of High, Medium, or Low. She had a column for mitigation strategies for how they would deal with it if the risk became an actual issue.

"I categorized each risk mitigation based on whether we would do something to avoid the risk, whether we would take steps to mitigate it if it does happen, or just accept the risk.

"That's cool. How often will you refer to this?"

"At least once a week," Holly replied. "Usually before a status meeting, I review them and try to see if there are any new ones or if the likelihood has changed. I always have to be on the lookout. And sometimes a risk actually happens, which turns it into an issue. In that case I'll need to decide whether the mitigation plan is valid and figure out what to do about it."

"Well it sounds like you're on top of risk management," said Emily. "Now I'm ready to get on top of some lunch. Are you ready?"

Holly started to grab her jacket when her cell phone rang. "Hold on a second, Emily." Holly answered the phone. "Hello… Yes, this is Holly. Oh yeah, I remember you Chad, how are you? Sure, that would be nice. Okay, I'll see you Saturday."

Holly hung up her phone and saw a wide grin appear on Emily's face.

"Who is Chad?" Emily asked.

Holly smiled. "I'll tell you all about him at lunch."

Lessons Learned

Tip #17 – Think like a pessimist for risk analysis

As a manager, it's best to have a positive outlook. It is more productive and sets an excellent example for the team. The one exception to that rule is during risk analysis. When assessing anything that can possibly go wrong, it's a good approach to view things in as negative of a light as possible.

Assuming the worst is the best way to identify risks. It's important to switch to a more realistic approach when assessing the likelihood and mitigation strategy.

Tip #18 – Develop a formal risk-tracking tool

All risks identified should be tracked in a tool. This can be as simple as a spreadsheet or a SharePoint table. Having the ability to sort and filter the list is a big plus. The tool should be easy to understand and available to view by all stakeholders

Tip #19 – Identify risks early and often

Holly had the risk analysis meeting with the team early in the project. But she's not done there. For the remainder of the project as she prepares for each status meeting, she will review the list to report the most likely ones or any risks that require executive awareness.

She will also review the list frequently to assess whether the likelihood has changed or if new mitigation strategies are appropriate. She will brainstorm on a regular basis to determine whether there are any new risks.

Chapter 6 – Meeting Fail

The first business requirements document (BRD) was scheduled to be complete at the end of the week and Holly had scheduled a formal review of it with the business users. The BRD covered a lot of business rules and she wanted to make sure she elicited feedback from as many of the business users as possible. Twenty-seven people were invited and she reserved the company's largest conference room.

On the day of the meeting she had coffee and bagels delivered. She projected the document on the wall so everyone could see it clearly. People started arriving a few minutes prior to the scheduled meeting time. The start time came and went as people gathered around the table selecting refreshments. Ten minutes after the meeting was scheduled to start, only about half of the invitees were present.

Holly announced to the crowd that they would be starting soon, but she wasn't sure who heard over the dull roar of the crowd. People were still trickling in. She finally got people to start taking their seats after about fifteen minutes.

The meeting started almost twenty minutes late. After a brief introduction and overview of the project, they began going through the requirements. The document was thirty pages long and she hoped to get through the full document in the two hours allotted. That meant they would have to go through it swiftly.

They hadn't gotten far into the document before Holly recognized they were in trouble. Although the document had been sent out in advance, it was clear that most of the attendees were viewing the document for the first time. There were questions about why certain decisions were made and the group rehashed issues that had been resolved weeks ago.

With only thirty minutes left in the meeting, they had only gotten to page nine. Holly announced a time check and told the group that they needed to speed things up if they were going to make any progress on the requirements review. That resulted in only a slight speed up. There were still questions coming from various attendees at each bullet point in the document.

When the time was up, they had only gotten about halfway through the document. Holly told the group that she would schedule another session to get through the remainder of the document. After everyone left, she felt defeated. She had hoped to get through the whole document so that they could make updates and get the approvals they needed to meet their deadline. Another meeting would set them behind schedule.

After they cleaned up the conference room, Holly sat down with Emily and released her frustrations. "That, my friend, was a disaster."

"Yeah," said Emily. "I didn't think it would take that long to get through one document. Some of those people had no idea what this document was about. We sent the document out so they would review it. I can't believe they didn't even look at it."

Holly nodded her head, "That was really frustrating. I'm going to head out. I've got dinner plans with my mom tonight. I don't think I'd be able to focus on any work anyway."

Holly sat across from her mom at Amigoni's Ristorante, listening to her talk about the latest production issues she was experiencing at the bicycle factory. As the waitress set two glasses of wine in front of them, Ann turned to Holly and asked, "How is your project going?"

"Today is probably the wrong day to ask," she said with a look of chagrin.

Ann gave her a sympathetic smile, "Rough day?"

Holly told her about her meeting fiasco and her frustration with the fact that no one had even reviewed the document prior to the meeting.

Ann sat and listened closely to Holly's story. Thoughtfully rubbing her hands together she asked, "How many people did you have in the meeting?"

"Twenty-seven were invited. Twenty-three showed up."

"That's a lot of people for a meeting to review a document. Was it necessary for each of them to sign off?" her mother asked.

"Not really," Holly answered. "I was trying to include more people to make them feel part of the solution."

Ann thought for another moment to gather her words. "I think your intentions were good. It's always good to get as much buy-in as possible. But it sounds like there were two problems. First, no matter how far in advance you send the document to the meeting participants, very few of them are actually going to read it. Too few to assume you'll breeze through it in the meeting."

"I suppose you're right," Holly answered.

"Second," Ann continued, "I've found that the more people you invite to a meeting, the harder it is to keep it from going out of control and the longer the meeting will be. Everybody has to get their two cents in and it spirals out of control."

"So what would you suggest I do?" Holly asked her.

"Here's what I suggest. Schedule another meeting but only invite the people necessary for signing off on the requirements. Then, schedule enough time to go through the document as if no one has read it. If that's four hours, so be it. Tell them that it may not take all of that time if you get through the document faster, and that it will go faster if everyone reviews the document ahead of time. That will give them some incentive to read it if they can make the meeting go faster."

Holly nodded in agreement. "That all makes sense. I wish I had done that in the first place."

Ann smiled. "You'll know next time." She opened her menu. "Let's order. I'm hungry."

The next afternoon Emily swung by Holly's office. "I'm making updates based on the feedback we got in the first part of the BRD yesterday. I'll have the document ready by tomorrow. I'm going to add a matrix at the end of the document where we list all of the people that need to sign off on the document. I was just wondering who to include on the list."

Holly thought for a minute and said "That's a good question. Let me check with the user team and get back with you."

When she worked for Harrison Foods, she knew all of the necessary players for reviews. With so many new players resulting from the merger, she wasn't quite sure who to include.

That afternoon as she was walking by Sam's office, she stuck her head in. "Hi Sam, I had a quick question for you. Who do you think we should include on the review list to sign off on the business requirements?"

Sam looked like he was expecting the question. "Have you completed a RACI matrix yet?"

"A what?"

"I think you just answered my question. Do you know what a RACI matrix is?"

"I've seen a few racy movies, but I didn't think *The Matrix* was one of them," she said, smiling.

Sam laughed politely at her awful joke and pointed his hand toward the chair, inviting her to take a seat. He walked up to his whiteboard and drew a large rectangle, adding horizontal and vertical lines to create several rows and columns.

He started to explain, "A RACI matrix identifies the roles and responsibilities for various tasks for all of your stakeholders." He listed names of some key stakeholders for the project along the cells in the first column. In the cells along the top row he wrote *Bus. Requirements, Status Report* and *Architecture diagram.*

"RACI is an acronym for Responsible, Accountable, Consulted, and Informed. So for each task listed along the top you want to identify the responsibility for each person listed in the first column. For instance, Erica is an owner of the business team. What is her responsibility for the business requirements?"

Holly thought for a few seconds and said, "She should definitely sign off on the requirements document."

"OK, if she signs off, doesn't that make her accountable?"

"Yes, I suppose so."

Sam put an *A* in the cell that intersected Erica's name and *Business Requirements.* "OK," he said. "What about Emily? "

"I would say she's responsible, right?"

Without answering, Sam wrote an *R* in the cell for Emily. "What about you?" he asked.

"Would I be consulted?" she answered, uncertain of herself.

"No," Sam said. "Consulted means you provide input for the information. I would say you need to be informed."

They continued on through the cells to complete the matrix on the whiteboard. Sam explained that some people may have no involvement with some documents and their entry would simply be *N/A* for not applicable.

Task	Bus. Requirements	Status Report	Architecture diagram
Erica	A	I	N/A
Emily	R	C	I
Holly	I	R	I

"Once you've completed it," Sam said, "you can refer to it for any document you need to create. You'll know who is responsible for completing the task, who is accountable, who should be consulted to provide input, and who simply needs to be informed."

Holly looked at the example they had just completed. "This would be helpful in identifying all of the roles and responsibilities on the project."

"What I recommend," Sam continued, "is that you list all of the major tasks and deliverables for the project in the first row. Then list all of the major stakeholders of the project in the first column. You may need to go through the process of filling in the matrix a few times. You should review this with each of the stakeholders to insure their agreement. It's especially important that those who are responsible or accountable are on board."

Holly went back to her office and completed the RACI matrix. She then reviewed it with all of the stakeholders. With that completed, she had a much better understanding of the roles and responsibilities of each stakeholder on the project.

She scheduled a follow-up review of the BRD, inviting only those that were designated as accountable and responsible. They went through the entire document in the allotted time and she obtained the sign-off she was seeking.

Lessons Learned

Tip #20 – Limit meeting invitations to the necessary people

The more people that are invited to a meeting, the more discussion you invite. Discussion in and of itself is a good thing. But when too many people are vying to have their voices heard, the amount of input becomes overwhelming and unmanageable.

It is best to limit the number of people to the essential attendees. If there are others who may benefit from the outcome, invite them as optional attendees, but make it clear to them that meeting minutes will be kept and provided to all invitees, whether they attend or not.

Tip #21 – Learn from your mistakes

The first requirements review session didn't go well for Holly. She realized that she invited too many people to the meeting. This contributed to the meeting starting late and enabled too much input and feedback in the meeting. She learned that she needed to reduce the number of people to the critical few that should provide input.

Following Ann's advice, Holly's second attempt showed that she had learned her lesson.

Tip #22 – Create a RACI matrix

A RACI matrix makes all responsibilities clear to the project manager and all stakeholders. When stakeholders know their responsibilities upfront, there should be no surprises when the project manager expects someone to review or sign off on a deliverable.

Chapter 7 – Estimating the Effort

With the Business Requirements Documents signed off by the business users, Holly sat down with Kyle and Paul, the architect and tech lead, to begin reviewing the final requirements with the goal of providing high-level estimates.

She provided both of them with a list of all of the tasks for the project. As they sat down with her, she introduced it with the underlying goal. "This is the project backlog document. You have each had a chance to review the BRDs and discuss them with the business analysts. Now we want to break down the work into logical components and develop high-level estimates for each one. These won't be final estimates. Those will be done by the actual developers. I want to get a level of effort estimate from you today."

Holly led them through the first major section. It was functionality for one of the main web pages that order entry users would use to start an order. Kyle and Paul discussed it for a few minutes and agreed that their estimate for this page was 160 hours.

Holly was uncomfortable entering estimates to the plan for items with such a long duration. "Can you break this item down into smaller components? If this is really four weeks of work, I'd like to break it down into more manageable components so we can track progress easier."

"Not really," Kyle replied. "It just takes that long to do it. What makes you think it's unmanageable?"

"Normally, when you run late on a task, it is not known until you're approximately halfway to three-quarters through the estimated time. If you run late on a four-week task, how soon will you know you're behind?"

"Maybe not until later," said Kyle, "but it's just too hard to break it down any further."

Holly threw Kyle a skeptical look. "Talk me through what is involved in this 160-hour task."

Kyle glanced at Paul, who provided an explanation. "This web page goes to several database tables in the system. There are many variations from the scenarios based on whether the customer is a premium, preferred, or select level customer."

"What is the most common customer level?" Holly asked.

"Most are preferred customers," Kyle answered.

"So what if you broke this down into these components?" Holly said. "First, create the base page as it works for all customers. Then create database connectivity. Then, develop for the preferred customer scenario. Once that works the way you expect it to, develop for the premium scenario and then for the select scenario. Why can't each of those breakdowns be estimated separately?"

Kyle wanted to argue but couldn't come up with a logical argument. "I could probably do that," he said a bit reluctantly.

"I'd like you to break down each one to components of less than forty but no less than four hours. Anything less than a half a day will use unnecessary time to manage," Holly said.

Kyle and Paul spent the next fifteen minutes breaking the item down into smaller components. When they finished, they had created five sub-tasks, each with estimates of less than forty hours. They reviewed each one with Holly.

"What is your margin of error?" Holly asked.

"We really don't have a margin of error," Kyle said. "We know that we'll be over on some estimates and under on others. We usually build in enough contingency time to allow for the times when we underestimated. Over the course of the project, they should all even out."

"Did you add contingency to this estimate?" Holly asked.

"No," said Kyle. "We add that in after all the estimates are totaled up."

"Rather than add contingency," Holly countered, "I would prefer that you provide a range for each item. An optimistic estimate if you assume very few issues that will set you behind, and a pessimistic one where you assume almost a worst-case scenario. That way, we can plan for times somewhere in the middle. We can also track how often we go over and determine whether there is a trend causing some tasks to take longer.

"This is also a more transparent way to communicate it to the business users," Holly continued. "For each task, when we give them a best- and worst-case scenario and list the assumptions for each, it allows them to help us avoid certain obstacles and get our tasks completed sooner." She pointed to an item on their list. "For this thirty-six-hour task, is this estimate the best-case scenario?"

"Well, no," Kyle replied. "The best case is probably something like thirty hours. If everything went fine, we'd be able to do it in three and a half days. We padded it a little to allow for issues."

"So there is contingency built into the estimate for each component as well?"

"Well…yes, a little," he stammered. "But we almost always use it."

"What happens when you don't?" Holly asked.

"We end up using any extra time on some other task. It almost always evens out."

"It's still misleading to the business owners," Holly said. "In order to be as transparent as possible, we should set some assumptions for both ends of the range so that they know what to expect. You told me the fastest you can develop this page is thirty hours. Make that your low-end estimate and list all the assumptions for what would have to occur for that to happen. Then give me an upper range for your worst-case scenario estimate. The thirty-six hours plus whatever other contingency you would have to add with assumptions around the likely delays that could occur – sick days, systems go down – things like that. Then, if those things happen, the business people know what to expect and how much the task will be delayed."

Kyle and Paul went back to work on their estimates. They spent another ten minutes talking about assumptions and developed an estimate range for each of the five components they had previously defined. They went back to Holly to review the updated estimates.

"You provided a range of sixteen to forty hours," said Holly. "So tell me under what conditions it could be sixteen hours and what conditions it would take a full week?"

"That's simple," Paul replied. "If everything goes well and there are no obstacles that stop the programmer from moving forward, it will be sixteen hours. But, if we run into obstacles, the worst-case scenario is forty hours."

Holly thought about this and asked, "What are the obstacles in the worst-case scenario that push it out to forty hours?"

"It could be anything," Paul replied. "The data team doesn't deliver the test data in time, the infrastructure team doesn't have servers ready, or maybe the business comes back with new requirements."

Holly paused to gather her words. "We have risks defined for those first two items, so those are covered. Also, if the business comes up with new requirements, it will result

68

in a change request. We have procedures in place to handle any of these situations. So you're telling me that if none of those three issues occur, your programmer will be able to develop this code in sixteen hours?"

"Not necessarily," Kyle said defensively. "It could end up being more complex than we think. It's still just an estimate."

"So if none of those issues you mentioned occur, what's the worst-case scenario for it being more complex?"

Kyle and Paul studied the figures for a few moments, making notes in the margin of the sheet. Kyle finally said, "I would say that it could increase by as much as four or six hours."

"Okay," Holly said rubbing her hands together. "Since we have tools in place to handle delays in data, infrastructure, or new requirements, the estimate range for this task is sixteen to twenty-two hours?

"Uh, yeah, I guess so," Kyle replied.

"Alright, I'll send you a list of all of our identified risks. Please review the list. For any more estimates don't add anything into your ranges to allow for those risks. We already have mitigation strategies for them."

Kyle and Paul nodded in agreement.

"I have one other question," Holly said. "I see that your estimates are in terms of hours rather than days. Assuming everyone works eight-hour days, if I divide these estimates by eight can I assume that will be the estimated number of days for development?"

After a moment of thought Kyle responded. "No, not really. For this sixteen-hour task, I think it will take the programmer three days. He has to develop the framework first, which will take eight hours. Then we need the deployment group to deploy it, which usually requires a one-day lead time. Once they complete the deployment, he can finish the content piece which accounts for the other eight hours of work."

Holly nodded in understanding. "So what we have is three separate tasks, all of which are interdependent. We need to break it down like that so the deployment team knows what they need to do and when they need to do it."

Kyle nodded without looking at her.

Holly continued. "So let's give this task a duration of three days and create a task for the deployment group. They need to know the dependency. Whoever does the programming for this can plan to work on another task during the day when they are waiting for the deployment group."

Kyle and Paul went through the entire backlog, breaking the larger tasks into smaller components, estimating each item with a logical range of hours. Once that was completed, they made another pass through the list and determined actual durations for each item.

At the end of the day, they presented the list to Holly, who was very happy with their result. "This is exactly what we need for tomorrow's iteration planning session," she said.

Holly had dinner with Chad that night. She found that she was enjoying the time they shared together more and more as time went on. Chad had an appeal that made him interesting and fun. He shared a lot of his knowledge with her from his own experiences, but she never felt that he was being condescending or acting like a know-it-all. They would talk for hours about other shared interests outside of their work lives.

On this evening, though, she wanted to pick his brain. She had her first iteration planning session the next day. She had done her homework and had a good general idea what she would do, but she thought getting advice from a seasoned veteran like Chad couldn't hurt either.

Chad gave her some tips, but primarily told her that she and the team shouldn't forget the driving principles of agile development. "'Agile' is another word for 'rapid and limber.' It's supposed to create an environment where you can quickly produce a product, show it to your customer, get feedback, and adjust accordingly," he said. "If the customer doesn't like it, it isn't right. This approach allows you to find that out in time to make adjustments rather than after the project is finished."

The next morning, Holly introduced the meeting. "Welcome to our first iteration planning session," she said, launching what was to be a new approach to project work for many on the team. While most of the team had been working on projects that planned all of the work from a large project plan that would be performed over several months, Holly introduced the principles that Chad had taught her about the agile approach.

She introduced the team to the use of four-week iterations, or sprints. "Every four weeks we'll meet like this and review the business requirements that we expect to complete over the following four weeks. We'll distribute the programming and testing tasks to the appropriate individuals based on your skill level, write them up on sticky notes, and plan them out on the wall chart right here in our team room." She pointed to a section of the wall that had each team member's name down the left side and the dates for each day of the next four weeks along the top.

Holly led the team through each step in the process. Emily and her business analysts presented an overview of all of the business requirements for the four-week iteration. Then Holly instructed the developers to go through the project backlog that Kyle and Paul had created. "Go through this list and identify tasks that are required to complete the work for this iteration. Then, transfer each task to a sticky note with an estimate that you can commit to and fill out the four-week schedule."

The development team had been at work on the tasks for about an hour when Grant came up to Holly and said, "I've finished my estimates. Should I start putting them up on the wall?"

Holly answered, "I want you to be able to commit to these work efforts. When you put a number down, can you commit to the whole team that you can make these estimates?"

Grant looked at her. "I think so," he said. "But anything can happen."

"Working under the assumption that there's not an earthquake and you don't get sick and all kinds of external occurrences like that can you commit to that estimate?"

"I think so. Should I pad my estimate?" Grant asked.

"No," Holly protested. "Make sure you understand what is involved and then put down a number of days that you can commit to getting it done. If you find out it will be harder than you anticipated, you may need to put in some extra time to get it done to meet your commitment. If you finish it earlier, you can start on your next task earlier. The point is that this should be more than just an estimate. You should be able to commit to these dates. "

Grant went back and conferred with his teammates. They discussed what was involved with each task. When the team was finally ready to put the tasks on the planning wall, they all felt confident about their numbers -- confident enough to commit to them.

Once the team had placed all of the tags on the wall, Holly stood and reviewed the final product. It had been a successful planning session. Now she would have to teach the team how to provide daily updates on status.

72

Lessons Learned

Tip #23 – Provide a confidence range for estimates

Estimating is generally more art than science. No one can predict the future and know what kinds of obstacles will cause their best-laid plans to go up in smoke. When a project manager provides single-value estimates to stakeholders, it sets an expectation that the team will meet that estimate.

Providing stakeholders with a high and low range and explaining the assumptions around both ends of the range, gives the business team a better idea of what to expect. It also provides visibility regarding the types of obstacles that cause delays. If some of those obstacles are caused by the business users, they may be more willing to respond to requests faster in order to speed up the project.

Tip #24 – Follow the 4/40 estimating rule

Long task estimates of forty hours or more should be decomposed into smaller tasks to make them easier to manage and track. If someone falls behind on a task, it's better to know sooner rather than later.

Tasks should be manageable on the low end as well. Albert Einstein famously said, "Make things as simple as possible, but no more." Anything smaller than four hours should be combined with other small tasks so that the overhead of management is not a time drain.

Tip #25 – Discourage contingency in estimates

The purposes of risk analysis is to make all stakeholders aware of what could happen and to define mitigation strategies for handling those risks if they become issues.

Contingency for estimates should not include additional time to mitigate risks. The difference between the high and low of an estimate range essentially becomes the contingency – extra time allowed for margin of error.

Tip #26 – Clarify between estimates based on time and duration

Project estimates are often made in terms of hours. However, there are often delays within the task for transfer to another team member or to obtain feedback from someone. Once the number of hours have been determined for a task, it is best to determine the duration in days to take into account how long the task is expected to take from beginning to end.

Tip #27 – Have team members commit to their own deadlines

Although technical leadership can provide high-level estimates to give a project manager an idea of the expected level of effort for the work as a whole, the actual estimates should be provided by the team members who will perform the work. The team members' estimates should be numbers that they are willing to commit to.

When team members provide their own estimates, the technical leads should be prepared to push back and challenge them to make sure the estimates are not aggressively low or so high that they will always undercut the estimate.

Chapter 8 – Standing Up

The next morning at nine o'clock, the team assembled for their first daily stand-up meeting. "Good morning everyone," Holly said. "We're going to meet like this every day. It shouldn't take more than fifteen minutes. We'll go around the room and everybody will provide three pieces of information: What you accomplished yesterday, what you plan to accomplish today, and any obstacles blocking you from that plan. If there are any issues you need resolved, you can bring them up as an obstacle, but we won't be solving those problems as part of this meeting. Does everyone understand?"

Everyone in the room nodded and she began. "Yesterday, like everybody else, I was in the iteration planning meeting. I've put tags on the wall for all the meetings I have scheduled for the next four weeks and for the days I'll be out of the office. I'll continue to update it as my schedule is updated. Brandon?" She gestured to Brandon, who was on her left.

They went around the room with each person giving their updates.

Sam was there and Holly was happy to see him getting involved. Sam planned to join the meeting about once a week, not so much to get the status updates, but to gauge the mood of the team. He knew it wasn't all that important this early in the project when the stress was low, but he knew that if he made it a regular practice, it wouldn't seem so strange to the team during the high-stress periods when he wanted to get a real assessment.

About halfway around the room it was Eric's turn. Holly knew Eric was one of the best programmers on the team. She had selected him based on his attention to detail. Unfortunately, that attention to detail resulted in his status update taking about three times longer than anyone else in the meeting.

"I'm going to work on the data model this week and I have some questions about the fresh foods tables." Eric turned to Danielle, the database administrator, and said, "Danielle, I need you to provide the table relationships for me to move on."

"What do you need?" Danielle asked.

Eric was standing in front of the whiteboard in the conference room. He grabbed a dry-erase marker and started drawing some squares and arrows. "I need to know the relationships –"

"Wait a minute! Time out!" said Holly, forming a T with her hands. "You guys will need to take this offline and discuss it between the two of you. Remember, if you have any obstacles that you're facing, bring it up and make arrangements to meet later. Eric, it sounds like these table relationships are an obstacle and that Danielle is the person to help you remove that obstacle. You two should meet after we're done here."

Eric set the marker back in its metal tray and meekly said, "Sorry."

"I'm not trying to scold you," Holly explained. "But we don't resolve the issues in this meeting; we just identify them so that we know which ones we need to resolve for the day."

Everyone nodded and Grant took his turn. He was brief, to the point, and didn't once touch the dry-erase markers.

Continuing around the room, Brett took his turn. "I worked on the development of the distribution portal page yesterday after our planning session and it's done now. I plan to start on the detail page right after this meeting."

"What do you mean when you say the portal page is done?" asked Holly.

Brett paused. "Uh...I'm just done. What else can it mean?"

"So you've created test data and unit tested it? And you've deployed it to the QA environment for the quality assurance team to test it?" she asked.

"Yeah, I mean... no. I finished coding it, and I tested it, but I haven't created any test data," he said.

Some of the team members chuckled, realizing the lack of logic in his last comment.

"How did you test it without test data?" Holly asked.

"Well I was able to bring up the screen without any issues," Brett said somewhat defensively.

"Okay, so the screen is code complete, but it's not done. You can't call it done or mark it off the board until you've created test data, unit tested it, deployed it to the QA environment, and informed the QA team that it's ready to test," Holly instructed. "I want to make sure every developer hears that and understands that. I'll repeat, code complete is not *done*. Unit tested is not *done*. It's not *'done done done'* until you've completed all of those steps and it's in QA's hands. Any questions?"

There were a few nods from the developers and Holly noticed a few smiles from the QA team members.

"Brett, how long will it take you to get the portal page done?"

"I can create some test data and test it this morning. I can probably have it ready to deploy to QA by mid-afternoon."

"That's great," Holly said. "Once you do that and deploy it, make sure you notify the QA team by e-mail. Then you can mark off that tag on the board."

Brett nodded in agreement while the other developers on the team added notes to their to-do lists.

The meeting, which was scheduled for only fifteen minutes, ran for nearly a half hour.

Sam noticed that as everyone gave his or her update, Holly questioned each team member for additional detail or suggested ways to better accomplish their tasks. In one instance, she reminded the team member of something they had already mentioned they were planning to do.

When Holly finally thanked everyone for their updates and the team began to disperse, Sam followed Holly back to her desk.

"How did you think that went?" he asked.

"What, the meeting? Oh, I thought it went well," she replied.

"It seemed to go a little longer than planned. Was there more conversation than you had planned?" Sam prodded.

"We have a lot of issues to tackle and that's the only time we're all together to talk," Holly answered.

Sam was hoping that his not-so-subtle questions would lead Holly to realize why he was asking, but she wasn't taking the bait and he had to run to another meeting. "Ok, why don't we do lunch? Do you have plans?"

"No. That sounds good."

One thing Holly liked about having lunch with Sam was that they ate at nicer restaurants than she normally frequented when she paid herself. She smiled as they sat down at Dmitry's. She loved the food there and it was quiet enough to talk.

After they placed their orders and exchanged some personal stories, Sam dove in to his ulterior motive. "I wanted to ask a few more questions about this morning's stand-up meeting."

"Did you think there was a problem?" Holly was finally starting to get his drift.

"Oh, not really a problem, I just thought it want a little long. Stand-ups are meant to get quick updates to share with the team. I thought the updates, and as a result, the meeting, went a little long."

Holly nodded, "They're supposed to be about fifteen minutes, but sometimes they're just going to go long. I tried to stop Eric from going into too much detail. And I needed to explain to Brett for everyone's benefit that he wasn't really done. Do you have any other suggestions?"

Sam was happy to get a solicitation for advice. "I thought the way you handled Eric and Brett were appropriate. But I noticed that you asked a lot of questions of the other team members. Do you worry that they aren't giving you enough information?"

"I just like to make sure I've got everything," Holly said. "Sometimes different people don't tell the whole story. And I want to make sure they understand the whole task so that they get everything done. I just don't want anyone running behind."

"Oh, I can understand that" Sam agreed. "One of the hardest things I had to learn as a young manager was trusting my team to do their job."

"Well I do trust them, I just like to make sure everything gets covered."

"Understood, but when you verify details and remind them of things that they have already mentioned, it can give them the impression that you don't. I've found that sometimes it's okay to let them fail, especially when you meet on a daily basis. If they fall behind in one day, it's not so hard for them to catch up. If they fall behind frequently, it warrants a little more involvement."

"You think I'm micro-managing them?" Holly asked in a concerned tone.

"No, I just think it's just a good idea to balance your management approach for the appropriate times. If they seem to be doing all right, let them give their updates and move on. If they miss something or have some exception situation, then probe a little deeper. That gives them a little more rope. If they hang themselves with it, then you simply hold them accountable."

Holly thought about it and realized that what Sam was describing was exactly how he managed her. Whenever she was running behind on her tasks, he kept a closer eye. If she was on target, he gave her a lot more leeway. She decided she would try that approach. But first, she was going to order dessert.

Lessons Learned

Tip #28 – Keep the team focused

Stand-up meetings are intended to be quick and focused. Each participant should tell the team what they accomplished in the previous day, what they plan to accomplish in the upcoming day and anything that is blocking them from those accomplishments.

If there are issues that require input from other individuals, it is inappropriate to try to resolve those issues in the stand-up meeting. Instead, the individuals whose input is required should be called out so that a follow up conversation can be arranged.

Tip #29 – Agree on the definition of 'done'

It is the project manager's responsibility to ensure that everyone understands when they are completed with their tasks. Any follow-up tasks such as testing or verification should be spelled out so that the assigned team member knows everything involved with completing the task. Follow-up communication to any downstream team members should be defined also.

Tip #30 – Have a balanced management approach

Management styles can be hands-on, where the manager gets involved with minor details and wants to be involved with every decision or hands-off, where the manager wants very little detail and only wants an update when things go off-course.

When managing a large project, the presumption should be that the team members are professional and can make some decisions on their own. If a team member is very new to the job, they may require additional monitoring. Otherwise, trust the team members and allow them to do their jobs. If they fall behind, it can be identified in a daily stand-up meeting and corrected before they fall irreversibly behind.

Chapter 9 – Staffing Decisions

"Is there a problem with our estimates?" Kyle asked Holly in her office.

"No," Holly answered. "Not directly, anyway. I just realized after reviewing your estimates that after this iteration, we may need more developers."

Holly went over the plan with Kyle. After a few minutes of analysis, Kyle said, "You're right. If we want to get all of this done by June, we won't be able to do it with our current staffing plan."

Holly nodded. "I'll go through our preferred vendor list to get a look at résumés for some available developers."

Three vendors responded to Holly's request, each submitting résumés of several developers. She and Kyle determined that they would need three additional developers on the team. She scheduled interviews with six of the candidates. She planned to meet with each one for about thirty minutes. Then Kyle would interview them for an hour.

Before the interviews were held, she sat down with Kyle. "What are you looking for with these developers?" she asked him.

Kyle gave Holly a half shrug. "We're just looking for good strong developers," he responded.

"Okay," she said. "We're going to interview six developers for three positions. What if they're all 'good strong developers'? What specific skills and attributes are we looking for that will distinguish the three best candidates?"

"What do you mean?' Kyle asked.

"For example," she continued, "I would like them to have some experience working in the consumer products industry. We specified that they should have at least three years of experience as developers. Do you have some specific database experience or other technical requirements?"

Kyle thought for a few seconds. "Well, it would be good if they had experience with HTML and JavaScript. And they should probably be pretty deep with SQL database experience."

"Okay, there we go." Holly drew a matrix on the whiteboard. She wrote the column header *Candidate Name* in the first column. She then listed each of the attributes they wanted from their candidates in each of the following column headers. In the *Candidate Name* column, she listed the name of each candidate that they would interview. "I'll type this up for each of us to use," Holly said to Kyle. "For each candidate you interview, give them a grade from one to ten in each attribute. This will allow us to make sure we're focused on the right criteria in each interview and that we evaluate each candidate fairly against the same criteria."

Candidate Name	3 years' experience	Consumer Products Industry	JavaScript Experience	SQL Database Experience
Richard				
Mary				
Andrew				
Deepthi				
Jack				
Lisa				

After interviewing all the candidates, Holly and Kyle met to consolidate their findings into a master evaluation matrix. They sorted the list by their total scores and discussed each candidate at the top. They selected the top three to sign contracts with. Based on their findings, Holly was confident that they had the group of developers that best fit their needs for the project.

Once Holly and Kyle decided upon the three new developers they wanted to add to their project team, she called the vendor, Logi-Tech, to work out a deal with them. Each of the developers had a published billing rate of $120 per hour. Holly felt that she could get a lower rate if she were to bring on three developers.

She spoke to the sales rep, Mark Jewell. She liked Mark. They had done business before and they both shared the same birthday, so he always remembered to call her and wish her a happy birthday. Mark was pleased to hear that she liked three of his developers. "That's great news. When would you like them to start?"

Holly knew that the earliest she could get them was in two weeks, but she wanted to create an air of urgency for Mark. "I'd like them to start tomorrow."

"Well, as I told you when I sent you the résumés, we need at least a two-week notification and it's still subject to their availability."

"True," Holly answered. "But I started talking to you over two weeks ago when you pulled the résumés together. I thought the clock would have started running at that point."

"We don't start that two-week clock until we know which consultants you're going to take. That gives us time to give a notice on their current contracts."

"Well when will these developers be available?" She asked, with just a bit of fake exasperation in her voice.

Mark checked for each of the developers and said, "I can have one of them available a week from Monday. The other two can be available the following Monday."

"Ouch. So if I want to have them all start together for training, I have to wait more than two weeks?"

"Well, you can get Andrew earlier than that," Mark said. "Can't you train him that first week and then train the other two the following week? These are smart people. They're not going to need all that much training."

"I'm sure they're smart," Holly replied, "but I need them to come up to speed on the business. It's just more efficient for me to train them all at once. Since I'm getting three people, can you bring their rates down any?"

"I'm afraid not. We can start giving volume discounts once you take six or seven developers. But I can't cut the rate anymore with three. You know how paper-thin our margins are."

"I'm sure. But we're getting these developers for an extended period of time. I'm also waiting longer than I planned for them to start."

"What kind of a discount were you thinking about?" Mark countered.

"I was hoping to bring it down to closer to $100 per hour."

Mark laughed. "I couldn't do that even if you had twenty developers."

"How much would you cut the rate for six developers?" Holly asked.

"If you were to take six developers, I could give them to you for $115."

Holly knew that adding three more developers would not reduce the duration of the project for her. She had room to add one more to her staff efficiently. She did some quick calculations and determined that if she added one more person and reduced the rate for each developer by five dollars, she would have a good deal.

"I'll tell you what," she told Mark. "If I take one more developer, four in total, would you reduce my rate to $115?"

"I'd have to have you take a couple more people in order to do that," Mark answered.

"Okay," Holly said, implying concession. After a pregnant pause she said, "I've got some candidates I want to talk to at Access Development Partners. I'll let you know if I still need these people."

Mark paused. He didn't want Holly to go to his competitor. Finally he said, "Holly, I can't discount these people if you only take four people."

"I understand," she replied. "I'm just under a pretty tight budget."

They said their good-byes and hung up. Although Holly had every intention of calling Access Development Partners, she liked the quality of people that Mark provided at Logi-Tech.

After lunch that day, Mark called her back. "I spoke to my boss. We really value your business, Holly, and we want to continue that. If you'll agree to take four developers, we can bring the rate down to $116 per hour."

"When can they start?" she asked.

"I have Andrew available next Monday, I can have the other three start two weeks after that."

That gave Holly time to train a trainer to help her with the remaining people. "When can you have a contract ready?" she asked.

"You'll have the papers on your desk tomorrow morning," Mark replied.

Holly hung up satisfied that she had worked out a good deal with Mark and was getting some good quality developers.

Holly sat at her desk on Monday morning, a little tired from a busy weekend. She was deep in thought preparing a summary of hours for the next day's status report when a sudden ring from the phone startled her for a moment. She saw that it was the security desk downstairs; she couldn't believe that she had forgotten all about it.

"Hello?" she said, as if not knowing what to expect.

"I have Andrew Franklin here to see you," the disinterested voice on the other end responded.

"Yes, please tell him I'll be right down." Holly sounded calm on the call, but she was panicking on the inside. She had completely forgotten that Andrew would be starting on the project that morning. She gathered her thoughts as she rode the elevator down to the lobby.

"Hi Andrew," Holly greeted him. "It's good to see you again."

"Good morning, Holly. How is your morning going so far?" Andrew asked.

Holly didn't dare tell him the truth. She escorted him to her office and quickly checked her schedule. She had a few meetings and debated about taking him with her, rationalizing it as a training experience.

Once she was able to get him to the human resources department for an hour to complete the required forms, she talked to Emily about spending some time with Andrew while she was in meetings. For the rest of the day, Holly scrambled and improvised to gradually begin getting Andrew up to speed at Harrison-Lee Systems. She felt bad that she left him to read documentation for much of the day. Over the next few days, she showed a little more preparation, arranging for some meetings with key project team members to work with Andrew and help bring him up to speed appropriately.

Realizing that she had three more developers starting the following Monday, Holly resolved not to make the same mistake twice. She developed a checklist for on-boarding new employees. It was a checklist of things she should have had ready for Andrew. She made arrangements in advance with the people she wanted to speak with the new employees and she had security badges, cubicles, and laptops ready for use as soon as they arrived.

While she was at it, she created a similar checklist for departing employees. Many of the tasks were the undoing of the on-boarding tasks. But she wanted to have a checklist ready when an employee left the project.

Two weeks later, Holly wasn't surprised by the calls from the security desk and her new team members were up to speed on the project quickly.

Lessons Learned

Tip #31 – Know your resource needs before interviewing

When hiring to fill a position on your project, it is common to interview more candidates than you will hire. It is important to identify all of the skills that you would like in the ideal candidate. Chances are you will not find a candidate that has all of the skills, personality traits, and knowledge you desire. But preparing a score sheet with a prioritized list of skills and experience allows an interviewer to evaluate each candidate with common criteria. This helps to identify the best candidate or to narrow it down for a final round of interviews with a short list of candidates.

Tip #32 – Sharpen your negotiation skills

Most project budgets are limited. Whether acquiring additional staff members or new hardware or software, good negotiating skills are a must. Determine the highest rate you can afford for anything you acquire. It's also important to try to determine the lowest your counterpart will go. Identifying a value between those two values will help ensure a win-win solution for both sides.

Tip #33 – Integrate team member roll-ons and roll-offs smoothly

When a new employee or consultant starts on your project, the first impression you give that person may establish how their entire experience will be on the project. It is important to be prepared for new team members so they feel welcome and begin being productive as soon as possible. It is equally critical to roll them off of the project just as smoothly. This makes their exit smooth and makes the entire team more productive.

Creating an on-boarding checklist of tasks to prepare for new employees can ensure a smooth transition on to the team.

Chapter 10 – Planning the Chaos

Holly leaned back in her chair, studying her schedule for the day. She was attending two important meetings that morning. She planned to get all of the information she needed to develop a first draft of the project plan.

Her first meeting was with Erica, who represented the user community. In that meeting, Holly told her that the project would need a dedicated full-time user to help with their user acceptance testing.

"We're actually working on hiring one now," Erica said.

"How long do you think it will take to hire someone and bring them up to speed?" Holly asked.

Erica considered the question for a few seconds and replied, "I hope we can get someone within three weeks. It should take another month to have them up to speed."

Holly made a note of the seven-week lag time to have someone from the user community ready to test.

In her second meeting that morning, she discussed the infrastructure needs for the project with Kyle.

Kyle showed Holly a spreadsheet detailing the number of servers that his team had determined would be necessary to meet the capacity needs of the newly combined company.

"We'll need approval from the finance group for an expenditure of this size," Holly said, reviewing the list. "How long do you think that will take?"

"For this amount the financial approval process should take no more than three weeks," Kyle said. "Once we receive approval, it takes about two days to get the order processed to the vendor."

Holly wrote these time frames down. "How long does it take the vendor, once they receive the order?"

"On average, about six weeks. For an order this big, it could take up to eight."

"Are there any factors that could cause a longer delay?" Holly asked.

Kyle thought for another moment and responded, "If they have to back-order components, it could take several more weeks."

Holly took down more notes.

"We should also add a task in the plan to clear out an area in the server room for the servers we request," added Kyle. "We can do that once we get approval, I would create the approval as a dependency."

"How long will that take?" Holly asked.

Kyle thought for a moment. "About a week," he replied.

"Do you need to wait for the approval? Couldn't you start clearing the area once you submit the request?"

"Yeah, I suppose we could," responded Kyle.

That afternoon Holly updated her project plan based on the information she gathered in her meetings. She entered lag times of three weeks for the approval of the servers and two days for processing the order. She entered additional lag times of seven weeks to hire a full-time user for testing and another eight weeks to allow for the server order to be processed.

Since they could start clearing an area for the servers as soon as the approval request was submitted, she entered a lead time for the overlapping start-to-start dependency with the financial approval.

She added reminders in her calendar to check the status with each group on a weekly basis to verify that each of the scheduled tasks was on track. She wanted to make sure adjustments were made to the plan at the first hint of a delay in either activity.

Once Holly had entered all of the tasks into the project plan and accounted for all of the dependencies, she did a first pass at assigning the tasks to the most logical people on the project. When she was finished, she took a look at her resource allocations.

She immediately saw a problem. There were weeks where Brett was allocated for over two hundred hours, while Eric had only four hours' worth of work. The problem was that Eric didn't have the right skills to do many of the tasks that were assigned to Brett.

She reallocated some of Brett's tasks to Brandon, who had some of the same skills. She was able to reduce Brett's allocation some, but he was still over-allocated by thirty hours across two weeks. There was no other alternative to assigning the task. She decided to spread his tasks out further.

This extended the project timeline a bit, but she didn't have much choice. Brett was the only person with the business knowledge and technical skills on the team to do many of the tasks.

Holly referred to the notes from her meeting with the quality assurance team. In that meeting, she had asked the team to review the requirements and provide estimates for developing test scripts, test data, and perform the test execution. After reviewing the numbers one more time, she entered the estimates in the project plan.

The next day, she sat down with the Erica again to review the draft of the project plan. Erica had few questions until she got to the section for testing.

"We've never had a project with that many hours dedicated to QA," said Erica.

Holly nodded, "In past projects that I've managed with Harrison Foods, we have consistently run late because of the number of bugs found by the QA process. On top of that, once we went live, we found a lot of bugs in production. It's a lot more expensive and time consuming to fix, retest, and make emergency deployments to production. It's always better to find the bugs earlier. I surveyed some of the Lee Foods team members and found that they have a history of doing the same thing."

Holly showed Erica a slide that provided statistics from a major think tank showing that the number of hours dedicated to QA during the QA process was about fifty percent lower than the number of hours spent after production. "You can see that putting the hours in early is the most cost effective," she added.

Erica found it hard to come up with an argument for spending the hours earlier rather than once they were in production. She leaned back in her chair and allowed Holly to continue.

Lessons Learned

Tip #34 – Attack planning as a process

As Holly began to plan her project, she knew she needed to gather all of the tasks required to complete the project, have them completed in the proper sequence, and document the appropriate dependencies. To do that, she needed to follow a process. This process included:

• Defining all the tasks for the project.

- Obtaining estimates from each team performing those tasks.
- Identifying the skills required for each task.
- Determining the duration of each task based on the number of people who will perform them.
- Considering lead times for any tasks that need to begin earlier in the plan.
- Defining dependencies between tasks and sequencing them accordingly.
- Developing the timeline.
- Identifying gaps in the plan and ways to compress the plan including tasks that can be done in parallel.

There will always be changes to the sequencing and new dependencies that require adjustments to the plan. But planning in a systematic approach allows the project manager to create the baseline plan, making any subsequent changes minor.

Tip #35 –Understand and manage lead times and lag times

There will be tasks in the project plan that have lag times. These are tasks that require a wait time while they process. Items with a lag time should start as early as possible to allow for the task to complete quickly. On Holly's project, hiring a new user and bringing them up to speed and processing the server order represent tasks with lag times.

There may also be tasks with lead time. Tasks with lead time can overlap other tasks. Since clearing the server room can be done while the financial approval is taking place, it has a one-week lead time.

Tip #36 – Understand the types of project dependencies

Many tasks in a project plan will have dependencies where one task is dependent on another in some way. There are four primary types of dependencies for tasks on a project.

- **Finish-to-Start (FS)** is the most common type of dependency. This occurs when a dependent task cannot begin until a preceding task has been completed. For example, when the team is ordering new servers for the system, they cannot place the order to the vendor until they have signature approval from the finance team. The start of placing the order is dependent upon the finish of the finance approval.

- **Start-to-Start (SS)** means that a dependent task cannot begin until another task has started. An example of an SS dependency is once the hardware order is placed, the team can begin the parallel task of clearing space in the server room for the new equipment. The SS dependency is most often used when tasks can be performed in parallel.

- **Finish-to-Finish (FF)** dependency is created when two tasks must finish together. An FF dependency can be established when two teams are working toward the same deadline. For instance, while a development team is working on writing code for the final product, the quality assurance team is busy developing test scripts which will be used to test the completed code. If they plan to finish at the same time, test execution can begin when they are both complete.

- **Start-to-Finish (SF)** dependency requires a dependent task to start before another can be finished. This is most commonly used when tasks must overlap to insure continuity. An example of this is when new servers are purchased to replace legacy servers. When the task of installing the new servers has been started, the task to power down the legacy servers can begin.

Tip #37 – Level your resources

When planning a project, it is the project manager's goal to plan as many tasks as possible in parallel. Unfortunately, some tasks can only be performed by specific people with specific skills or processed through a single machine. In those cases, the project manager must single-thread the tasks to be performed sequentially.

The project manager should perform the due diligence to determine which sequence makes the most sense based on dependencies that other tasks may have. It may make the most sense to perform the shortest duration tasks first.

The project manager should always try to determine whether alternate resources can perform the tasks, including the option of going outside the company. Can a contractor be hired for a short period of time to perform the task earlier? Can a machine be rented in order to perform the task in parallel?

If no other options can be implemented, it may simply result in a later finish date for some tasks.

Tip #38 – Plan for quality

A proactive approach in project planning is to allow extra time for quality assurance. If a system goes into production that has not been properly tested, errors that are identified during production will be more costly to fix.

Additional costs of poor quality are reflected in poor customer service and lost customer loyalty. Planning additional time for quality always pays off in the long run.

Chapter 11 – A Little Schooling on Status

olly looked around the conference room table at her team leads on an early Monday morning. She asked them about their weekend and shared some small talk before jumping in to business. When she felt that everyone was settled in and ready to start the week, she announced, "I have my first status meeting tomorrow with Sam and the business stakeholders. It will be a standing meeting every Tuesday. In order to prepare, I want to meet with you each Monday to get updates that I can't always get from the daily stand-up meetings."

She went around the table asking each team lead some specific questions regarding the status. When it was Paul's turn, he reported the tasks that his team had accomplished over the past week and discussed the tasks they planned for the upcoming week. As part of his accomplishments, he reported that he had submitted requests to the four business groups that he reported to directly, asking for their feedback on several proposed changes from the IT team.

"Did you give them deadlines for their responses?" Holly asked.

"Yes, I asked them to reply by the end of this week."

"Can you forward me the e-mails that you sent them?"

"Uh…sure," replied Paul. "I sent four separate e-mails though."

"That's fine," Holly said. "Just send me each of them from your Sent file."

As Holly continued around the table getting updates from the others, she sensed some irritation from Paul. When she adjourned the meeting, she asked him to stay back for a minute. After everyone else had left the room, she asked if he was upset about something.

"I was a little confused by your request for those e-mails I sent to the business units," he said. "I got the feeling you didn't believe me. Don't you trust me when I give you my status?"

"Oh, I trust you," Holly said. "But I like to verify some of the more important things. My preference would have been that you copied me on those e-mails. That does two things. First, it lets me know that you sent the requests and how they were worded. Second, it lets each of the business units know that I'm aware of your request. If they don't reply in time, I can follow up by replying to your original request. It becomes kind of an implied escalation when you copy me."

"Okay, I'll try to include you more often. I just didn't want to fill up your inbox unnecessarily," Paul said.

"That's fine," said Holly, "but I want to clarify this trust issue. I trust that you sent the e-mails. It's more about me having visibility. This happens in business every day. Everybody from the lowest level to the CEO has checks and balances to make sure someone else verifies what they do. Believe me, Paul, I trust you to do your job and I'm not trying to micromanage you."

"Thanks, Holly. I appreciate you talking to me." Paul seemed to feel a little better once Holly explained it to her.

Holly stepped onto the elevator and pressed "three." Now that she had status updates from her team leads, it was time for her to finish her own status report. She approached the task with a bit of apprehension. Her task was to report the status of one of the organization's highest profile projects to her boss, the CIO, and several business stakeholders. She wanted to make sure she reported as much information to them as possible to give them an honest assessment of the project's status.

Stepping off the elevator onto the third floor, she heard a voice from down the hall that was unmistakable. She cringed at the thought of him interrupting a good day.

"Whatcha doin?" Pete asked, as if he was addressing a friend.

Holly faked a smile. "Oh, just getting ready to put my status report together."

"Just write 'Going down the tubes' and you'll be done," he joked.

She glanced at him slyly. "Oh no, you'll have to do your own status report."

He forced a smile in acknowledgement. "Make sure you raise the issue of Ben's project wanting the corn products financial reports changed."

Ben Singler was the head of the corn products division. That division was facing intense pressure over recent bad press for poor nutritional value of their products. Sales had been gradually lagging over the past several months. Ben had requested additional data on sales of corn products to get a better idea whether there were specific demographics causing the drop.

"That's just an initial request from Ben," Holly countered. "Nothing has been approved and there is no indication it will be part of this project's scope. I don't see the need to escalate it to the management level yet."

Pete smiled his typical condescending smile. "Take my advice. The sooner you let the management team know about it the better. They don't like surprises. What do you think will happen if you wait to tell them and he gets the change approved? You're going to have to tell management about a new change that's been approved and you need to add it to the scope of the project. They won't be happy that you're springing it on them late."

When they parted ways, Holly debated with herself whether to include the issue. She knew that management didn't want or need to be made aware of every tiny issue affecting the project. She thought that this was, at best, a risk. But even as a risk, she didn't see the need to escalate it.

She thought about Pete's advice that the management team doesn't like surprises. Pete always put things in such incontrovertible terms. After deliberating on it, Holly decided it was safer to include it in the status report as an issue.

Sitting down to compile her report, she reviewed tasks in her project plan and updated her status report with items that had been completed over the past reporting week. After proofreading it thoroughly, she sent it out to the management team to give them time to review the document prior to the meeting.

Holly looked out the window. The deepening twilight of the late autumn evening made her realize how late it was. It's time to go home, she said to herself as she closed down her laptop for the day.

The alarm went off at six o'clock. Holly's eyes opened with one immediate thought: Tuesday is status day. She was a little nervous. The meeting itself was a formality. She would meet with the management team, review the status, and probably end the meeting within fifteen minutes. But she felt a little edgy leading up to it.

At one minute before ten o'clock, she sat waiting patiently in the empty conference room. She had the room and the projector ready. Soon Sam walked in followed by Steve and Jennifer, members of the business team. Erica called into the conference bridge from her home office. Holly had her status report projected on the screen. After a minute or two of small talk, she began discussing the status.

Her status report was five pages long and included information about business requirements, all of the open issues and risks, as well as details on staffing levels.

"The past week has been eventful," Holly announced. She proceeded to list all of the activities they had performed the previous week, including the kick-off meeting and a few other meetings that were held.

She continued, reciting the tasks from the project plan that the team had accomplished over the past week:

- Completed requirements document A-7
- Met with QA team to plan testing approach
- Provided feedback to Infrastructure team on server needs
- Scheduled meeting with security team to discuss security roles in new system

After listing off each item, she asked if there were any questions. There was a momentary pause and finally, Jennifer raised her hand with a somewhat puzzled look on her face. "Holly," she said, "I'm a little unclear regarding what these things mean. I mean, I understand each one of these at a high level, and it looks like we're making progress, but it doesn't tell me whether or not we're on track."

Holly was a little confused. "Well, these are tasks out of the project plan. You all have access to it in the project repository. I'm just updating you on tasks from the plan that have been completed over the week."

Erica's voice came out of the speakerphone. "We understand that, but most of us don't have the time to review the detailed project plan on a weekly basis. Seeing these tasks helps us to see the specific things getting done. What we'd also like to see is how we are progressing each week in a way

103

that's a little more meaningful to us. Is there a way that you could provide some way of saying, 'We're supposed to be here and we're actually here'?"

Holly looked at Sam who was not saying anything but taking some notes. "Sure," she replied. "I'll see what I can do."

No one had any further questions or comments and Holly shifted the discussion to the issues section. She started by discussing the "Ben report." Erica was the first to question why this was an issue. "When did Singler request this report?"

"I just heard about it yesterday," Holly admitted.

"Has it been approved by anyone in IT?" Sam asked.

"No. From what I know about it, he just submitted it. I just had it here to make you aware that it had been requested," Holly said.

"This isn't an issue. This isn't even a risk at this point. Let's move on," said Erica trying to get the meeting over with.

Holly was half pissed-off at Pete for his stupid advice. The other half she reserved for herself for listening to it. She decided that she had to ignore Pete in the future to avoid embarrassment.

Holly continued reviewing the long list of project issues when Sam stopped her.

"Holly, are you asking us to assist you in resolving these issues?"

"No," Holly replied. "I just want you to be aware of the issues we've been addressing over the past week."

"Well that's fine," Sam answered back. "But we have access to the issues log if we need to see that kind of information. It would be more efficient if you just brought to this meeting the issues, risks, and other concerns that require our attention. I would expect you to be able to address all of the other items by yourself. It's not that I don't want to be bothered with this amount of detail, I just don't want to be bothered by this amount of detail," he said with a wry smile.

Holly smiled but was a little embarrassed. She assumed that they would want to know as much detail as possible about such an important project. But he was telling her that she was providing too much information.

After Holly had gone through the remainder of the status report she asked if anyone had any questions. Erica spoke up over the phone line, "Last year I was involved on a project that Pete managed. His status reports provided a lot of statistical information like cost variance and cost performance index. I was wondering if you planned on using any of those statistical analyses in your reporting."

Holly paused for a split second, focused on not rolling her eyes. "I'm familiar with those approaches for reporting status. I just don't think they're effective measurements."

"How so?" Erica asked.

Sam nodded at Holly in both approval and encouragement to go on.

"Statistics like that can be manipulated, especially for development efforts. You'll see later in the project where I provide percentages and other statistical numbers for our progress for testing, because that effort lends itself more to statistical analysis. If we have fifty test cases and twenty-five of them have passed, I feel comfortable saying that we are fifty percent through test execution. I'll also provide statistical tracking for the defects we identify during the testing process. Showing the number of defects open versus how many our developers are closing shows a fairly accurate picture of our velocity to close defects."

"Why doesn't that type of statistical analysis work for other phases of the project?" Erica inquired.

"When you talk about requirements and coding effort, it's much more ambiguous," Holly went on. "If you're writing a requirements document, how do you know if you're fifty percent done? You don't know how many pages the document will be until you're done, so you can't just say, 'I've got ten pages written so I'm halfway done.' There's a lot of analysis time involved too, so you can't just base it on the number of pages you've written."

Sam joined in. He and Holly had discussed this before and they were both on the same side of this argument. "If you ask a developer for his percentage complete they generally will tell you based on how far they are into their estimate. If they said it will take them eighty hours to complete and they're forty hours into the effort, can you guess what they will tell a project manager when she asks for his percentage complete?"

There were a few smiles from the team at his rhetorical question.

Sam continued. "Instead, we ask the business analysts and developers to estimate small chunks of work of no more than about three to five days' effort. That way, if they get behind on a task, we know within a day or so. We can reassign or reprioritize tasks to adjust, rather than getting two weeks into a task and finding we're more than a week behind."

"As I look back, that makes a lot of sense," Erica replied. "When I saw all of those statistics, they always seemed to indicate that we were on schedule throughout the first part of the project, but seemed to fall behind in the later stages."

"The statistics can be misleading," Holly said. "We think it's better to talk in terms of value, and you can't determine value until something is actually delivered. Dividing tasks into smaller chunks shows the smaller packets of value and gives everyone better visibility into our progress than percentages complete."

"This makes sense," Erica said. "You should talk to Pete about this approach."

Holly nodded in agreement, struggling to keep from laughing. Sam just smiled and replied, "Yeah, I should probably do that."

Holly asked if anyone had any other questions. When there was an appropriate amount of silence, she thanked everyone for their time. She turned off the speakerphone and watched Steve and Jennifer leave the room.

Once they were the only ones in the room Sam turned to her and said, "Last week the check engine light came on in my car. So Saturday, I took it into my local repair shop."

Holly glanced at him in a way that indicated that she had other things on her mind, but Sam pressed on. "After running their computer analysis on it, they handed me a report that showed all of these compression volumes and other statistics on my engine. I looked at it but it might as well have been written in German. The numbers meant nothing to me. They sat down with me and told me what the value should be for each of the numbers. The bottom line was that I needed a new fuel pump. They could have told me that without showing me the numbers. But I thought that if they were going to show statistics like that to anyone who doesn't know anything about cars, they should also show me what the numbers are supposed to be. I didn't know if the number was high or low or just right."

Holly started to realize where he was going. "This conversation isn't about your car is it?"

Sam smiled. "Your status report was accurate. Everything you told us was true. But in many ways, it was like that computer analysis from my auto repair shop. For most project managers, the project plan is the world around which everything revolves. It allows you to track the completion status of every task on the project. But the project plan is simply a tool for you. Business users, executives and other stakeholders really have no interest in navigating through the detail of a complex project plan. It's your responsibility to translate the detailed tasks and data from the project plan into meaningful information that communicates to them how the past week's accomplishments affect each of them."

Holly looked at him intently. "This is what Jennifer was talking about; not understanding what the accomplishments meant."

"In your list of accomplishments you mainly listed activities. For instance, you listed a meeting. A meeting isn't really an accomplishment; it doesn't demonstrate to the management team that anything got done."

"What would you rather see?" Holly asked.

"What was the purpose of the meetings? Were any decisions made in them? You listed the kick-off meeting. We were all there so we knew that took place. But the real accomplishment of the kick-off was that we announced the project, the purpose, and the schedule to all of our stakeholders. In our Thursday meeting, we met with the architecture team. But I'd rather see the outcome listed here. I don't care that you met, I care that you were able to determine a design approach for the infrastructure. Do you understand what I mean?"

"I think so," Holly replied.

"In the weekly status," Sam continued, "the management team wants to know if we're getting anything accomplished. You could list twenty meetings, but if nothing gets accomplished or decided in those meetings, then you're just churning away without getting anything done. We want the accomplishments to show just that, not your to-do list from last week."

"I think I understand," Holly said. "I'll take a different approach next week."

"Thanks," Sam said. "And keep up the good work." He walked out and left her alone.

Holly sat there feeling discouraged. She wanted to make such a good impression and felt like she had been torn apart. She wanted to kick herself for listening to Pete, but that wasn't even the problem. She hadn't given a good status report and everyone knew it. She wondered how long it would be until Pete found out.

Lessons Learned

Tip #39 – Trust but verify

When Holly asked Paul to forward to her the e-mails he sent to the business, he felt that she did not trust him. In an effort to avoid micro-managing, many managers trust their team members to a fault. While trust in important, the effective project manager needs to make sure the team keeps them informed of communications with key stakeholders. Additionally, it helps to have the team member include the project manager on communications to add credibility to any deadline requested.

Tip #40 - Escalate appropriate issues to management

When reporting issues to an executive team, the issues should be limited to the issues where input or a decision is required from them. Reporting every issue the team has experienced to the executive team will overwhelm them with detail and give the impression that the project manager can't resolve the issues on his or her own.

Tip #41 – Report results, not activity

Executives view status as a chance to gauge whether the project is making progress. When completed tasks are listed from the project plan without any context of how it translates to progress, executives will become confused or frustrated with the uncertainty.

A much better approach is to show progress from a milestone perspective. Sometimes a graphical approach is effective. If the project manager can provide a graph or matrix that indicates whether targets are being met on a weekly basis, executives will have a better indication of whether the project is on track.

Tip #42 – Use meaningful performance measurements

As Holly mentioned to the executive team, statistics can be manipulated to indicate things the project manager wants to project rather than accurate progress. Executives tend to develop a comfort level with statistics thinking that numbers provide rock-solid evidence of whether a project is on track.

Instead, breaking large tasks into smaller, manageable chunks and reporting on their completion allows everyone involved to monitor progress in more meaningful terms.

Tip #43 – Communicate in the customer's terms

When working in heads-down mode, people tend to get caught up in the terminology and measurements that are unique to their role. Each level of management has a unique perspective and, with that perspective, its own set of terms.

Project managers need to make sure that status – and any other communication to executives – is given in terms meaningful to them. This allows them to consolidate it with additional information and make appropriate decisions.

Chapter 12 – Piling on the Doubt

As Holly tapped on the keyboard of her laptop, she heard a knock on her open door. Her eyes met Sam's and she smiled.

"Have you got a minute?" he asked.

"Sure," she said, holding out her hand to invite him to have a seat.

"I wanted to discuss this contract we're considering signing with Menlo Systems for data conversion," Sam said. "I want to make sure they are a company we want to do business with. I like their software. That's not the issue. My concern is whether they're stable enough to be a key stakeholder for this project."

"Stakeholder?" Holly responded with a confused look on her face.

"Well, yes," replied Sam. "They would be a vendor for a key software component on this project."

"I really just consider the central end users to be the stakeholders," Holly said. "The key stakeholders are the core user team that represents the remaining users."

"Oh, no," Sam replied. "The stakeholders group is a much broader group of people. Each vendor we deal with holds a stake."

"I figured they're just trying to make money off of us," Holly shrugged.

"Certainly they are," agreed Sam. "And we want them to so they stay in business. But I also want them to be interested in the success of the project. Hopefully they see that our success insures their success. But there are a lot of other stakeholders." He continued, "The whole IT team, including you, are stakeholders. They won't be users of the new system, but you're all definitely invested in the success of the project. Don't you see this project as an opportunity for your career?"

"Well sure, but –"

"I hope every member of your team sees it that way. They all have a huge stake in the success of Merge-Tech. What about the indirect users of the system? Not every employee here will physically interact with the system, but you're integrating it with Techno-pay, our external payroll system, right? Anyone who receives a paycheck at Harrison-Lee Systems has a stake in our success.

"Stakeholders include internal and external vendors, any government agencies that affect, or are affected by, our operations; even our customers, including the end customers that consume our products and the retailers that resell the products.

"A stakeholder is anyone that could be affected, directly or indirectly, by this project."

Sam had opened Holly's eyes to the importance of stakeholders. She realized that she would need to think in much broader terms when making sure that the needs of all stakeholders were addressed.

As the date for her first steering committee meeting approached, Holly became more and more nervous. This anxiety was out of character for her. She had reported to weekly status meetings many times in the past. But a steering committee meeting was a little different. She would be presenting not only to Sam, but to high-level executives in the company. Vice presidents would be there. The CEO was even invited. She had to be careful about what she reported and how.

114

When she worked for Harrison Foods, she knew her way around. It was a fairly structured hierarchical organization and she knew who reported to whom. More importantly, she knew who in the organization got things done. Every organization has a few people that get more done than their title reflects. Holly knew how to navigate within the hierarchy and outside of it to get to the right people that would cut through any red tape to get decisions made quickly.

She also knew who was connected to the corporate grapevine to give her the inside information she needed to allow her to make the right decisions.

With the new organization at Harrison-Lee Systems she wasn't so sure. Many of the executives from Lee Food Products took early retirement options when the merger was announced. And Harrison-Lee had been organized as more of a matrixed company. Many people reported to two different people based on the function they performed and the project to which they were currently assigned.

With all the new players from Lee Food Products and the new organizational format, Holly was confused. She wasn't sure where the power was. She never liked playing politics, but she knew it was important to know who the decision makers were.

She went up to Sam's office and saw Virginia, his administrative assistant. They had gotten along with each other whenever Holly came up to meet with Sam. Virginia also always seemed to have a good feel for what was going on within the company.

"How have you been Virginia?" Holly said. "How are you handling the merger?"

"Hi Hol, how's it going? I was wondering the same things about you? Are you gonna survive?" Virginia responded with a smile.

"Oh, I'm doing fine. I've got a steering committee meeting coming up in two weeks. I'm staying busy preparing for that, but otherwise I'm keeping my head above water."

"Who are you reporting to in that meeting?" Virginia asked.

Holly listed the executives from both companies involved in the merger, watching for Virginia's reaction to any of the names. She got down to Walt Roman and noticed Virginia raise her eyebrows.

"Do you know Walt?" Virginia asked.

"No, I've never met him," Holly answered. "I hear he's heading up the combined distribution team."

Virginia leaned forward and lowered her voice. "He's the heir apparent to be the CEO. Jim Feldon, the CEO of Lee Food Products was grooming him to take over at Lee before the merger. They were the two-man team that architected the merger. Feldon and the Harrison Foods CEO, Rob Adams, are only going to be co-CEOs for an interim period until things start to take hold as one company. Then they both plan to retire and Walt will be installed."

"Very interesting," Holly thought aloud.

"He also wants to use technology as the strategic advantage," Virginia continued. "If you're making any recommendations to the committee he'll be interested in the ones that give them advantages using technology."

"I'm glad I came up here to say 'Hi' to you Virginia," Holly said with a confident smile.

Virginia gave Holly her most confident glad-I-could-help smile and waved her off like it was all in a day's work.

As Holly stepped onto the elevator, she thought about the valuable information that Virginia had just relayed to her. She felt a lot more prepared for the upcoming steering committee meeting. But just in case, she was going to take Virginia to lunch someday before the big meeting. Who knows what other information she may have?

Back at her desk, Holly resumed putting her presentation together. Having been with Harrison for seven years, Holly knew that management there didn't like confrontation and controversy. She kept that in mind as she prepared her report.

She reviewed her list of high-priority issues. The development for the sales tracking component was behind schedule because the sales team had cancelled three meetings that she had scheduled to define their requirements. Holly knew the sales team was not very engaged in the project. They felt that defining their business requirements was a waste of time; it took valuable time away from their job of selling. They didn't earn commissions by defining requirements.

Jennifer Henry, the vice president of sales and marketing, was on the steering committee. Holly knew if she publicly shamed Jennifer by bringing that issue up in the meeting that Jennifer would eventually find a way to pay her back some day.

Instead, she reported that she only had a slight delay in the sales component and that she was having trouble finding time to meet with the sales team. She believed that downplaying the issue's importance and taking responsibility for the delay was the best thing to do from a political standpoint.

When the big day arrived, Holly sat in the conference room watching the executives appear through the conference room doorway. There was a lot of anticipation in the room as every attendee was interested in seeing how the new company would conduct its business.

Holly thanked the executives for their time and began reporting her status. She summarized the accomplishments to date and the activities they planned to complete before the next steering committee meeting.

When she got to the agenda item to review the project issues, she mentioned rather matter-of-factly that the requirements for the sales component was a bit behind scheduled and moved on.

Before she could complete the next sentence, Walt Roman spoke up. "Why are you behind on the sales requirements?"

Holly paused for a moment. Although she had prepared an answer, she wanted to present it with care. "I've had some problems scheduling time with the sales team to define the requirements. But we're working on a time that works for all of us."

"What kind of problems have you been having?" Walt countered.

"Well, there are just a lot of schedules that we're trying to plan around."

Walt wasn't going to let it go at that. "How many other groups have you met with to define requirements?"

"There are seven business units in all, and we've met with the other six." Holly almost immediately regretted her brutal honesty.

Walt must have read the discomfort in Holly's face and turned to Jennifer Henry. "Jennifer, why has it been so hard for your team to meet with the IT group?"

Jennifer looked at the firing squad of executives staring at her. She didn't know Walt very well but was surprised at the confrontation in front of the group. "Well, the team is in the middle of the busy season and a number of our sales reps that are on the implementation team are traveling quite a bit," she answered.

She opened her mouth to say more, but Walt cut her off. "We agreed at the beginning of this project that everyone assigned to the implementation team from each business unit would make time in their schedules to do whatever was necessary to make this project successful. Do we need to assign different people on the team from sales?" "No, I'll make sure we have them at the next meeting," Jennifer replied, writing a note on her notepad.

Walt still wasn't done. "I know sales people. They focus on selling and think that's the only thing they're responsible for. They can't be bothered with timesheets, paperwork, or meetings that don't increase their commissions. They earn a base salary in addition to their commissions and that is supposed to cover their time on these non-sales responsibilities. I don't want them dragging their feet and holding the entire project back. Is that understood?"

There was a painful look in Jennifer's eyes as she replied, "Yes, we'll get the meeting taken care of this week."

"Thank you," Walt said. He then turned to Holly and said, "Let me know if there are any other delays like this from any of the business units."

"Thank you," Holly replied. She continued on with the rest of her presentation without issue.

About an hour after the meeting, Walt stopped by Holly's office and asked to speak with her. They sat down in a nearby conference room and he began to speak. "I had a long talk with Jennifer after the meeting. She's going to have the sales team ready to meet by Friday. There's one thing I need to know though. When you raised the issue, why did you make it sound like it was your fault?"

"Well," said Holly, "I didn't think it was appropriate to point a finger at one group in the steering committee meeting."

"That's what those meetings are for," Walt replied. "If you're having problems with a group and can't get it resolved yourself, you should escalate it to the management level. It seems to me that Harrison Foods didn't do things like that. But that doesn't get things done. You need to keep that in mind moving forward. The management team now knows they'll be held accountable. We won't be sweeping issues under the rug to protect others. Is that understood?"

"Yes. I won't let it happen again," said Holly.

"Good. Keep up the good work, Holly," Walt said as they walked out of the conference room together.

Once Walt was gone, Holly walked over to Jennifer Henry's office to apologize for exposing her in the meeting. Jennifer put up both hands to stop her. "No, it's not your fault, Holly. Walt made it clear that things are changing. I need to get a little more involved to make sure we stay on task. How about if we set up a meeting every two weeks to make sure we're providing you the information you need?"

"That would be great," Holly said with a relieved smile.

"If anything happens between those meetings, don't hesitate to come to me and let me know. I'll make sure it gets done."

Holly thanked her and promised to schedule biweekly meetings with her starting that week. She saw the culture changing in the company and liked what she saw. She decided she would schedule regular meetings with the head of each business unit to make sure they were informed and didn't get blind-sided in a future meeting.

Holly was surprised how quickly each business unit leader accepted her meeting requests. Some even added a note thanking her.

Walt was changing the culture and she was going to comply with all of the unwritten rules that it encompassed.

As she headed down the hallway back to her office, she saw Sam standing there waiting for her.

"This isn't a good sign," She said, half joking.

Sam didn't even smile. "You hired Logi-Tech to help with the programming effort didn't you?"

"Yes, they've provided us with three programmers."

"I just got an invoice from Logi-Tech. Have they been working a lot of overtime?"

"Yes. Everybody is. We've been under some tight deadlines and needed everyone to work extra hours," Holly replied.

"Well, I understand that," Sam said. "But we contracted them on a time and materials basis. We pay for every hour they work. This invoice puts us almost thirty percent over budget for the period."

"I didn't realize that. I just assumed we were paying the same rates for each company."

"Well check with them and see if we can change the terms of the contract. If that can't be done, you're going to have to limit the hours those guys work. They can't work more than eight hours per day at these rates. The budget just won't allow it."

Holly looked at the invoices Sam left on her desk. She couldn't believe she let that happen to the budget. She leaned back in her chair and closed her eyes, feeling the desolate loneliness of responsibility. I'm bound to do something right one of these days, she thought to herself.

Lessons Learned

Tip #44 – Know your stakeholders

Anyone related to the project is a stakeholder. It's usually clear that the business people who will use the final product are stakeholders. Most project managers realize that the team members implementing the final product are stakeholders as well.

But there are indirect stakeholders too. Business users who receive outputs of the final product are stakeholders. If

121

the team is implementing a payroll system, anyone who receives a paycheck from the system is a stakeholder. Vendors and any people involved in assisting the project should be viewed as stakeholders as well.

Tip #45 – Be familiar with the organizational structure

There are many types of organizational structures. Some are hierarchical with a clear definition of who reports to whom. Some organizations are matrixed, where an employee formally reports to one person, but also has reporting responsibilities to one or several other people, such as a project manager. Still other organizations have flat structures with informal reporting responsibilities.

It is important for a project manager to know the organization's structure and how to get things done within that structure.

Tip #46 – Learn the company's culture

A company's culture is comparable to the personality of an individual. Each one is unique. Some cultures are cooperative, where everyone naturally works as a team. Others can be political, where people keep score of the deeds and misdeeds of others. Still other cultures may be non-confrontational, in which employees avoid making waves and causing strife. A successful project manager must get to know the company's culture and figure out how to work successfully within it.

Tip #47 – Know how your vendors' payment terms affect execution

Some companies have standard payment terms with which they require their vendors to comply. Others have vendors that dictate varying payment terms. In either case, the project manager should be aware of the terms agreed to with each vendor. Additionally, knowing how changes like overtime will affect your payments to the vendor will help the project manager stay on budget for the project.

Chapter 13 – Communicating Like a PM

"Did you get my e-mail?" Holly glanced up to see Emily standing in her doorway.

"When did you send it?"

"About an hour ago."

"I haven't checked e-mail since before lunch. I'll check it in about a half hour," Holly said, checking the time on her laptop screen.

Emily looked at her quizzically. "You schedule time to read your e-mails?"

"Sort of. Instead of continuously monitoring my e-mail, I devote time twice in the morning and once late in the afternoon to check my e-mail. This helps me to focus on more important things without interruption during the day.

"What more important things?" Emily asked.

"Mainly communicating with the team," Holly answered. "I try to schedule no more than two to three hours of heads down work each day so that I make sure I allow enough time for communication."

"Isn't e-mail communication?" Emily asked.

"Sort of," replied Holly, "but that's not what I'm talking about. Ninety percent of what I do as a project manager is communicate. I'm in meetings giving status or presentations or I have people coming up to me with questions or seeking information. Another big part of the job is facilitating communication across team members. For instance, if I know that one task is dependent on another I need to make sure the assigned team member understands that when they finish that task, they need to let someone else know about it so that person will be able to start their task. This is something a project manager sees as obvious, but is not always apparent to the team member. It's also about giving the team access to me. They may not want to come to my desk and bother me when I'm busy. But if I make myself more accessible, they'll be more willing to bring something up."

Emily nodded, seeming to agree, although she didn't fully understand. She vowed to watch Holly in the future to figure out how she actually communicated as a project manager.

In the next day's stand-up meeting, three developers on the project reported snags in their development that were causing delays. This was one of the most frustrating things Holly experienced in project management. There was really nothing she could do to speed them up. They needed to work through their issues and figure out how to finish their assigned tasks. They had discussed the issues with senior developers, but the tasks were simply more complex and just took longer to do than they had originally estimated.

In the meeting, all three developers reported being even further behind than they reported the day before. Each of them was at least a week behind schedule and there were other people on the team that needed their tasks completed before they could begin their next task assignments.

Holly looked at the plan and tried to identify ways to rearrange the schedule, but there really were not any options that would save a significant amount of time.

Her weekly status report would turn from a green status to yellow, indicating that the schedule may slip if they can't make it up somehow.

Not wanting to wait until the following Tuesday to report yellow status, Holly stopped by Sam's office. As she approached Sam's office, she could see that he had someone in his office. When she got close enough, she saw Pete sitting across from Sam. She could tell they were just finishing up, so she hung around to wait until they finished.

As Pete walked out he seemed to look through her, not as if she wasn't there, but as if it didn't matter. She paused for a moment wondering what they were talking about.

"Hi, Holly. What's up?" Sam asked, dissolving her daze.

"Hi, Sam. Do you have a minute?"

"That's about all I have. I'm heading to a meeting that starts in five minutes."

"I wanted to let you know that Brett, Brandon, and Eric are all about a week behind on their tasks. Their tasks were a lot more involved than they realized when they made their estimates and they're waiting for some other groups to finish their work. They're putting in some extra hours to get through, but I don't think they'll make up the time before our dependent downstream tasks are scheduled to begin."

Sam thought about what she said. "What's the schedule impact?"

"Right now, it puts the whole project a week behind. They're all critical path items. We're going to try to make that up as much as possible with some additional hours, but as you know, too many additional hours can be counter-productive. If they start programming tired, they tend to make additional mistakes.

"Yes, we need to balance the overtime and be smart about it. Let me know where we stand by the end of the week. Thanks for letting me know."

Sam headed for the elevator and Holly went back to her office.

That night over a drink with Chad, Holly told him about seeing Pete and Sam talking.

"They could have been meeting for any number of reasons," Chad pointed out.

"I know it sounds paranoid, but I just got a funny feeling from Pete as he left Sam's office," Holly said sounding almost shaken.

Chad tried to set her nerves at ease. "Don't jump to any conclusions. Just because two people are talking doesn't mean they're talking about you."

That night as Holly lay in bed, she thought about Chad's words. She knew he was right, but there was something about the way Pete looked at her as he left Sam's office that made her uneasy.

Lessons Learned

Tip #48 – Communication is the most important task of a project manager

A project manager is responsible for many heads-down jobs. Project plans needs to be created and maintained, status reports created, and documents reviewed. But those responsibilities are less important than the need to communicate.

Face-to-face communications with all stakeholders is the key to the project manager knowing what is going on and letting others know where the project stands. Holly could have just as easily sent Sam an e-mail informing him that the project was behind. Even though he was short of time, she was able to hold a conversation with him to explain it, allow him to ask follow-up questions, and provide answers. As a result, he had better information and a better feeling that Holly was taking care of the issue.

Tip #49 – Be visible for your team

When a project manager spends her entire day working heads-down in her office, team members may be reluctant to bother her with issues or suggestions. Being available and visible to the team provides access, removing barriers that may limit communication from the team.

Tip #50 – Communicate bad news as soon as possible

Many project managers use the weekly status meeting as their only communication with management. Believing that there is no reason to raise unnecessary questions, they withhold all information – good and bad – until the status meeting.

They often don't realize that more questions are raised when they provide less information. Additionally, sitting on information until a scheduled meeting increases the risk of management hearing bad news from another source.

It's no fun to be the bearer of bad news. But it's even worse for management to hear it from someone else.

Chapter 14 – Some Quick Wins for Holly

Holly looked up to see who was knocking on her office door. As soon as she saw Emily's pale face, she knew it wasn't a social visit.

"Uh oh, what's up?"

"You're going to kill me," Emily said.

"Unlikely, but I'll make a final decision when you're done," Holly said wryly.

Emily sat down. "Do you remember when you asked about my task of ordering the Wi-Fi equipment from Granderson Technologies?"

"Yeah, you told me a couple of weeks ago that you placed the order," Holly said.

"Yeah, I did. But I realized today that I had never received a confirmation or any response from the order. I just followed up today and they told me they never received the order. They don't have any record of it."

"Ohhh," Holly said, her voice fading out as she realized the ramifications of not getting the Wi-Fi equipment on time. Did they tell you the lead time?"

"It's normally about six weeks," Emily said. "But some parts are back-ordered so it could take as long as twelve weeks. Then they need a week to install it all. We aren't going to have this stuff here in time for our testing."

Holly thought for a minute and said, "There have to be other alternatives. We talked to a couple of companies, didn't we?"

"I think so, but this was the lowest-cost vendor."

"Check with the next-lowest-cost vendor and see how long it will take them. Call Granderson and find out which parts are on back-order and find out how critical they are. Also ask them if there is an option to pay to expedite those items. Let's see what all of our options are," Holly said.

"You got it," Emily said, standing up.

An hour later, Emily stopped by with an update. "I called Thomas Technologies. They can get everything we need within eight weeks, but we'll have to pay $1,000 more than Granderson quoted us. When I talked to the sales rep at Granderson, she said the items can't be expedited and the back-ordered items are critical pieces. We can't start testing until the full package is here."

"Okay, thanks," Holly said. "I'll put that information in tomorrow's status report."

"You're going to tell them about my screw-up?" Emily asked nervously.

"I have to. I can't hide issues like this. There is a chance that we'll get the equipment on time, but if we don't, I'm not going to surprise them that late in the process."

Emily started to protest and Holly stopped her. "Emily, this is not the end of the world. It may delay the project or we'll have to overlap some tasks, which will add a little risk to the project. But we can't hide issues like this from the executive team. This is their project and they have a right to know. If it makes us look bad, we have to live with it."

"This makes me look bad, though. I screwed up and it's going to expose me."

"Emily," Holly said, "I could argue that it makes me look just as bad as the project manager. But it's not about protecting how we look. I'm going to tell Sam this afternoon so he's not surprised in tomorrow's meeting. Then I'll tell everyone else in the meeting tomorrow. If I don't tell them, they'll find out further down the road when the actual delays start. They're going to be disappointed tomorrow, but knowing things like this in advance is always better than finding out later."

The next day in the status meeting, Holly explained to the executives what happened with the Granderson order and explained the options they had with the two vendors. Sam asked a few questions regarding how the mistake occurred and Emily got a little nervous. After a little discussion, Sam thanked Holly for the update and said to keep him informed.

Next, Holly moved on to a new request from the users for notifications on low stock volumes. She explained the options of programming the change in-house or purchasing a software package. "We could also do it later, after we go live with the system in June," Holly explained. "There will be subsequent updates which can include this functionality. It just wasn't prioritized for the June release."

"We need to find a way to include this for June. This is absolutely critical," Erica pleaded.

"Well if it's that critical, we need to either determine what functionality can wait until a later phase or push the project date out," Holly answered.

While the team felt that the functionality Erica had requested was necessary, no one wanted to even consider changing the project date. After extensive debate, Erica spoke up, "Holly, you mentioned moving some functionality out beyond June to allow for this. What items would be candidates to move out?"

"That's a good question," Holly replied. "Let me ask about that. What is driving the June thirtieth deadline?"

"That's when the two organizations legally become one company," interjected Sam. "The company needs to be using a unified software system."

"So, we need to be able to process orders from the time the order is placed to the time it is fulfilled by June thirtieth, right?" Holly asked.

"That's right," said Sam.

"What about all of the reports we produce?" Holly asked. "What if we had a release at the end of July or even the middle of August where we provided the monthly reports after the system has been used for a month?"

Sam and the other executives looked at each other thoughtfully. Finally Sam said, "That's definitely a decision for the business folks to make, but it's something to think about."

Jennifer joined the conversation. "There are some reports we use on a weekly basis, but there are some monthly and quarterly reports that we could put off," she said.

The other executives agreed. Emily volunteered to schedule a report review meeting to determine which reports could be put off until after the June deadline.

"Assuming we can eliminate a few reports from the scope of the June deadline," Holly said, "we may be able to swap that work out to be able to work on the notification functionality."

As they left the meeting, Emily turned to Holly, "The Granderson issue went better than I expected."

Holly smiled at Emily. "That conversation would have been much worse if we had waited to tell them. Bad news is no fun to give, but the sooner you give it, the more time they have to prepare for it. Then if it all hits the fan later, they're not surprised."

Lessons Learned

Tip #51 – Be transparent

When there is potential for bad news, many project managers try to keep the information from upper management. They hope they can figure out a solution before any delays or other consequences occur in order to avoid getting management involved.

More often than not, the negative outcome arises and the bad news has to be reported to management in crisis mode. It is better to give the management team visibility early on. The project manager can inform them why an issue occurred and what is being done to resolve it. This puts the executive team at ease knowing that the project manager is handling issues. Additionally, when the issue becomes a crisis, they have had time to think about how to handle it in emergency mode.

Tip #52 – Executives don't like surprises

When the project manager plans to report bad news in a status meeting, it's always a good idea to notify top management prior to announcing the news in a public meeting. This gives the manager time to ask questions privately and plan a response to the group.

By telling Sam in advance, he had the time to formulate questions and potentially offer advice during the meeting.

Tip #53 – Include the business stakeholders in scope decisions

When new scope was introduced by the business stakeholders, Holly explained to them how it would impact the project if she tried to add it to the project plan. By laying out how it affected the project, she allowed the stakeholders to be involved in the solution and provide informed alternatives to resolve the issue.

135

Tip #54 – Learn how to prioritize

If everything is a priority, nothing is a priority. Holly was instrumental in facilitating the executive team's needs to ensure that the highest priority functionality is provided for their deadline. By making them realize that other components were lower priority, she was able to rearrange the scope and timeline to better meet the customer's needs.

Tip #55 – Understand drivers behind deadlines

Executives sometimes select an arbitrary deadline in order to fire up the troupes. When the date has been announced by an executive, it often must be met to allow the executive to save face.

In general, deadlines are good. They give the team a target goal to meet rather than meander through tasks without direction. But deadlines need to be realistic and meaningful. Causing a team to work excessive overtime in order to meet an arbitrary date is counterproductive.

A project manager needs to understand why a deadline is set in order to motivate the team and set priorities. Additionally, the project manager should try to determine whether the deadline is movable. In the late 1990s, the year two thousand (Y2K) work had an unmovable deadline. Date processing had to be able to handle the new century by December 31, 1999. Other project deadlines may be movable. For unmovable dates, the scope of the project can be negotiated to include what absolutely must be delivered for the selected date.

Chapter 15 –Staff Insights

When Holly woke up and looked out her bedroom window, she thought it was a foggy day. Then she realized that the abundant pallor was snow. She hadn't heard any news since early yesterday. She turned on her radio to hear that they were talking about a winter storm warning. School closings and long traffic reports followed and Holly knew today's commute would be a character builder.

After her shower, she checked the local TV station. They were recommending that everyone stay home, with a forecast of eight to ten inches of snow by noon.

Holly heard her mobile phone vibrate on the counter and saw that it was Sam. "Looks like a rough commute out there today," she answered.

"It sure is," Sam replied. "We're going to close down operations and have everyone stay home today. It's just not safe to be out there."

"I think that's a good decision. It looks like we're going to get hit pretty hard."

"Yeah, even if people made it in, they wouldn't be able to get home. Can you call your team and let them know?"

"Will do," said Holly. "Hopefully I'll see you tomorrow.

Holly started going through the directory in her phone to call the members of her team. She realized she didn't have everyone's number. She opened her notebook and wrote down every team member's name. There were fifteen team members and she only counted contact numbers for ten of them.

She went through her e-mail system to find e-mails she had received from a couple of the missing people in the chance that they might have their contact information in their signature. That snagged her a few more numbers, but she still had a few team members with missing numbers. She had already sent an e-mail to the full team, but she knew not everyone checked e-mail before leaving for work, especially when trying to get an early start.

She called the people on her list and was able to obtain the remaining numbers from the team members she talked to. With the remainder of her day free, she put together a spreadsheet with every team member's name and his or her contact number. Hopefully there would be no more snow days. But if there were, next time she would be ready.

The next morning, the major streets had been cleared and were more navigable. Everyone on the team made it to work safely.

Paul had scheduled an eight o'clock meeting that day in Sam's office. Holly could tell Paul was excited. He hadn't given them much information regarding the topic of the meeting, but he had piqued their interest. As the tech lead, he took great interest in his team's productivity and was always looking for ways to improve.

After a minute or two of small talk about the snowstorm, Paul started in. "I'd like to discuss an opportunity to use a new software development application. I've been doing some research on it for a while. I've also been discussing it with some former colleagues who have used it at other companies and they've had a lot of success with it." Paul went on to describe the application, trying to limit the number of technical terms. He also provided some statistics to show Holly and Sam the type of productivity improvements other companies had experienced.

Sam finally broke in with a question. "What type of learning curve would our development team experience with a new tool like this?"

Paul was ready for that one. "I've spoken to three development managers at other companies who have successfully implemented this. It requires developers with some C-Sharp and Java programming skills. Assuming they have those skills, they're usually up and running at about ninety percent within two weeks, and they exceed their original productivity by about twenty percent by the end of the third week of use."

"Those are impressive numbers," Sam countered. Then he turned to Holly. "How many of the developers on your team have those skills?"

"Well, I know Brett and Brandon have worked with Java, but I'm not sure how deep they are. We've got a mix of Java and .Net developers but I'd have to poll the team to get a true assessment."

Sam frowned. "It would be nice to have an inventory of each team member's skill set and how proficient they are in each. Not just for those two skills. It would be good to know how much experience we have as a team in all sorts of knowledge areas."

Sam asked Holly to find out how much expertise the team had in the two programming languages to help them make a decision on Paul's suggestion.

When Holly got back to her desk, she put together a list of all of the skills she knew were currently required on the project, leaving room at the bottom for the team to enter additional skills they might have.

She scheduled a face-to-face meeting with each person on the project to obtain the information.

In her first such meeting, Grant sat down at the conference room table with a confused look on his face.

"Thanks for agreeing to spend a few moments with me, Grant," Holly said.

"What's this all about?" Grant asked.

"Well, I'm not singling you out. I'm having a meeting like this with each team member. I want to get an inventory of the skills you have. I'd also like to get some feedback from you on what you want to get out of this project and if there's anything I can do to help you with it."

"I hadn't really thought about it," Grant said. "I'm just coming to work every day to get my paycheck."

"Grant, the Merge-Tech project could really help you advance your career goals. This is not only a high-profile project, we're working with some advanced technologies. Coming out of this project, you could get assigned to some of the most interesting projects at Harrison-Lee Systems."

"Well, that's actually got me a little worried. I don't have experience in many of those newer technologies. I knew the systems we had at Lee Foods, but I don't know much about all these new technologies," Grant said.

"Well, that's part of what this meeting is about, too," Holly said. "I want to know where we're lacking in skills as a team. You're not the first person to express this concern. There are some technologies where we'll need to bring in a trainer for a group of people. There are others where we only have one or two people who lack any knowledge. We'll probably either send them to an off-site class or give them some online training if it's appropriate. We know there are new technologies that you can't just come up to speed on your own. I need to determine where we need training and make sure everyone is given the tools needed to make the project a success."

Grant had a look of reassurance on his face. "I have to tell you, that I'm relieved to hear that. I was actually worried that this meeting was to take me off the project because of my lack of skill."

"Quite the opposite," Holly smiled. "We have no interest in setting you up to fail."

They continued to talk for another twenty minutes discussing the technologies they would be working with and where Grant felt he needed training. Holly held a similar meeting with each team member. She then developed a matrix that detailed each needed skill for the project and the gaps in knowledge for each team member.

From there, she planned online and classroom training classes to fill each gap and make sure everyone on the team was prepared to perform on the project.

In the process, she solicited each team member for input on whether they would like to develop more expertise in a skill or, if their skill was more advanced, their level of interest in continuing to use that technology.

She even planned some online training for herself on agile project management. This would be a career-defining project for her too and she didn't want to be left behind. Maybe when this was all over, she could teach Chad a thing or two.

With her skills quest complete, Holly knew she was better equipped to match tasks to team members appropriately, based on each member's level of expertise as well as his or her level of interest.

Lessons Learned

Tip #56 – Create a team directory

Whether the project manager needs to contact the entire team or a single individual, creating – and maintaining – a team directory with multiple ways to contact each team member can be invaluable. Additionally, it's helpful to create an e-mail distribution list that can be used to send a single e-mail to every individual on the team.

Tip #57 – Keep an inventory of team members' skills and knowledge

Task assignment situations, requiring the project manager to determine who is best suited for a task come up in nearly every project. Having an inventory of skills for each team member is a valuable tool to assist the project manager in efficiently assigning the right people to the right tasks.

Tip #58 – Identify training needs

It is rare for a project manager to have all of the skills needed on a team. Some of those skills can be developed while the team members work with other, more experienced coworkers. Other skills need to be developed in other ways. It is a good practice to determine knowledge gaps and plan the appropriate training and mentoring to fill those gaps to maximize productivity on the project. Asking team members what skills they would most like to develop can be a morale booster if the project manager can match training with needs as well as desires.

Chapter 16 – The Demo Debacle

Holly scheduled customer showcases at strategic milestones throughout the project for the dual purpose of demonstrating the team's progress to the management and user community, and to validate that the requirements defined by the business were implemented as they wished.

With the next development milestone only a week away, Holly gathered the team to begin determining the functionality they wanted to show to the business in the next showcase. Holly had a list of the functionality that was slated for completion for the current coding iteration. Her hope was to include all of the functionality in the showcase, but she knew that wasn't always realistic. If a large number of defects was outstanding on certain areas of code, they may have to remove that functionality from consideration until the next milestone when it was more stable.

As they proceeded through the list, the team seemed confident that all functionality except for one screen would be stable enough to demonstrate to the business team for the showcase.

They all agreed to meet again on Thursday to verify the stability before the showcase.

On Thursday afternoon, Holly reconvened with the team to review the readiness status of the components to be showcased the next day. The team leads all agreed that, save for the one screen that still had a number of outstanding defects, they could demonstrate the listed items.

The next day, Holly and her team went to the training room to set up for the demo. A previous meeting in their reserved room went until the end of the hour, so they couldn't begin setting up until their meeting was scheduled to begin. They had never used the projector in that room and it was a different model than they were accustomed to using. The business users waited patiently while the team took a few minutes to connect the laptop and project the image successfully.

The wireless network they normally used did not reach to the conference room they were in. They had to call the help desk to obtain a guest ID and password to access the network.

They finally started the demo fifteen minutes after its scheduled start time.

Holly introduced the team to the business community. Most of them all knew each other, but there were some new faces in the crowd. She provided a quick status update, listing the functionality that they would be covering and then turned to Grant and asked him to begin the demo.

Grant looked surprised, not knowing that he was expected to perform the demo. He took the seat at the laptop and began walking through the application. Since he was unprepared, he did not have sample data ready to give a proper demonstration of the software.

There were several false starts as he went to a spreadsheet to find data that would work for the demo. At one point, one of the pages he was trying to display failed, causing him to restart the application and try again, resulting in the same page failure.

Despite the team's assurance to Holly that the application was ready for demonstration, the business users walked out of the demo with concerned looks on their faces. This was their first opportunity to view a significant portion of functionality from the new system. In the space of an hour, their confidence in the development team had waned significantly.

After all the business users had left, Holly made an effort to speak calmly, though she was trembling with anger. "I thought you said all of this functionality was working."

Grant spoke up first in a defensive gesture. "I didn't know you expected me to do the demo. I would have had some test data prepared that I could have used."

"That doesn't explain the screen blowing up. How were we ready for a demo when a screen blows up in the middle of it?"

Grant shrugged spreading his hands. "That was a data issue. Since we didn't have orders in the database for that customer, it failed. Again, if I had known you wanted me to perform this demo, I would have had a script with a customer who had orders to give a nice presentation."

Holly glanced at him in astonishment. "Who else would provide the demo? You're the developer. Of course you're going to perform the demo. Our next showcase has to go better than this."

There was nothing more Grant could say. They walked out of the room without another word.

Holly went back to her desk and thought about what had just happened. She had just lost significant credibility with the business community. She needed to figure out how to earn back the business community's respect.

She began writing down what went wrong. Next to each item, she jotted down things she and the team could have done differently for a better outcome. By the end of the afternoon, she felt confident enough to reschedule another demo with the user community the following week. She just needed to get to work preparing the team.

"Are you ready?" Emily asked as she stuck her head into Holly's office.

145

"Yep, I was just getting up." Holly disconnected her laptop from its docking station and followed Emily into the conference room. The other four meeting participants were already seated with the demo application projected on the screen.

Holly sat down. "Thanks for coming everyone. I hope by the end of this meeting, we will have a good list of functionality for what we will present to the user team for our new checkpoint demo. But first, Grant, I want to apologize to you again for dropping that surprise on you in the last demo. I should have arranged it with you ahead of time. It wasn't fair of me."

Grant smiled in acknowledgement of her apology. Holly had already met with Grant personally and apologized to him. This time he was involved in the planning to give another demo to the users.

"Would you like to get us started?" she asked him.

"Certainly," Grant responded. Over the next twenty minutes, Grant presented the functionality that they had completed to date and was ready for the demo. Holly had occasional questions about how something would work once it was complete and Grant explained that they would only be able to show certain options as part of the demo.

When Grant finished, Holly asked the other meeting participants to imagine that they were the business customer seeing this for the very first time. "What would your response be?" she asked.

Emily spoke up first. "I think they'd be happy with this. It looks really sound."

"So you think we'll meet their expectations on Friday when we present this to business community?" Holly asked.

"Absolutely," Emily said.

"Well that's good. But how do we make it great? How can we give a presentation to them on Friday that will exceed their expectations?"

146

Grant frowned. "I don't know if there is any additional functionality we can get finished to include in the demo by Friday. We still have some finishing touches on this part of it that will push us."

"It doesn't need to be additional functionality," countered Holly. "Let's discuss other ways that we can exceed their expectations."

Over the next thirty minutes, the team brainstormed several ideas on the whiteboard and eventually narrowed the list down to an approach they thought would exceed the user group's expectations. Over the next few days, Holly and the rest of the team worked on coordinating the demo while Grant led the technical team on fine tuning the technical aspects of the demo.

At two o'clock Friday afternoon, the team was ready when the user community filed in. As they entered the room they saw that all of the seats were arranged in the center of the room, while each corner was decorated differently.

Holly started the meeting by welcoming everyone to the demo. "Welcome to the new Harrison-Lee Systems. As we consolidate these two great companies, it is critical that we all work on a consolidated technology platform that allows us to function as one company that takes the great aspects of both companies and assures that our final product is greater than the sum of the parts. Today, we have prepared a demonstration of our software to show you what we have completed to date. Please note that this is only a checkpoint. We won't have it in a finished state for several months."

She then directed everyone's attention to one corner of the room where two members of her team stood. Paul represented a Harrison-Lee sales rep and Emily was a customer. They performed a role-play segment where Emily placed a large order with Paul. He entered the order on his tablet device which was shown on the wall through the

147

projector. The users were able to see how orders could be placed in the field.

Holly then directed everyone's attention to another corner of the room. Dominic was sitting at a desk with a headset working on a laptop. His order processing screen projected on the wall as Holly described how the orders were being consolidated and processed. They were batched together and sent to the distribution floor.

The third corner of the room represented the distribution area. They had borrowed some signs and clipboards from distribution and hung them in that corner. Grant wore a hard hat and held a tablet with its screen displayed on the wall. He described how the orders were distributed based on item location in the warehouse as Brandon stood next to him holding a device that showed how the workers in the warehouse would pick items from the many storage bins.

Finally, Holly asked everyone to direct their attention to the final corner of the conference room where a cardboard cutout of a miniature Harrison-Lee Foods delivery truck stood. There, Brett and Eric acted as workers loading actual food packages onto – or in this case behind – the truck. Eric stood there with an electronic device scanning each package. The screen projected on the wall, showing how inventory was reduced and orders placed automatically when volume threshold levels were met.

At the end of the demo, the user group gave the entire team a standing ovation.

Afterward, snacks were served to the team of the actual food items that were ordered by the imaginary customer in the demo. Holly hoped that showing the full life cycle from order to delivery to consumption made the demonstration easier to understand and more memorable.

As the business users left the room, they commended Holly and her team for not only showing them the functionality of the system, but giving them a better perspective on how it would affect their employees and customers in each area.

After all the users left, Holly told each member of her team to give themselves a hand. They had not just given the users a demo. They had exceeded their customer's expectations.

Lessons Learned

Tip #59 – A customer demonstration is a performance. Rehearse!

When presenting a demonstration to business users, it is important to build confidence in them that you are building a quality product. Proving to them that you and your team are prepared is the first step.

The first step Holly should have done was to hold a "dress rehearsal" prior to the demo. Holding a meeting with her team at least two days in advance would have given them time to define roles and responsibilities and fix any issues that were identified.

Holding the preparation meeting in the same room that the demo would be held would have allowed them to familiarize themselves with the room and the equipment, allowing them to work out any technology glitches ahead of time.

Tip #60 – Wow the customer

Instead of simply presenting functionality to the business community, Holly and her team came up with a way to exceed the expectations of the business users by demonstrating how it would work in their everyday lives.

Presenting to the users in that format informed them, entertained them, and more than anything, allowed the users to envision how the system would work from their own points of view.

Chapter 17 – A Day in the Life

It was a cool spring morning but the bright morning sun made it feel warmer than it really was. Holly parked at the outer edge of the parking lot to extend her walk and get some fresh air.

She took the elevator up to the third floor and walked down the hall to her office. She turned on her laptop and headed to the break room for coffee while the computer warmed up.

Sitting down, she took a sip of coffee and began her morning routine. This included going through her e-mail inbox, reviewing her to-do list, and verifying her meeting schedule for the day. One of the e-mails she received was from Grant.

To: Holly Hewitt
From: Grant Stevens
Subject: In late today

Holly, I need to drop my wife's car off at the shop on my way to work today. I'm going to be about an hour late. I'll make up the time by staying late tonight. Sorry for the late notice.
Grant

Holly made a mental note to talk to Grant when she saw him.

In the daily stand-up meeting, Dominic and Eric both announced that they were behind on their tasks.

"What is blocking you?" Holly asked for either one to answer.

"We're both waiting for access to the customer database from the database administrator for that area," Dominic answered.

"How long have you been waiting?"

"I submitted the request a week ago today," Eric spoke up. "But they're busy so I didn't want to bother them anymore."

"They should have had it for you within a week. When did you tell them you needed it?" Holly asked.

"I requested it for yesterday," Eric said.

"I'll look into it," Holly said as she added the item to her to-do list.

Brandon's turn was next. He reported being on time and didn't report anything slowing him down. Holly couldn't put her finger on it, but she suspected something was bothering Brandon. For the last couple of days, he had been out of sorts. Just the tone in which he reported his status made her think something was different. He lacked his usual enthusiasm. She knew it could be any number of personal issues or even a lack of sleep. Either way, she wanted to get to the bottom of it.

When the meeting ended, Holly pulled Grant aside. "Hey, did you get your wife's car taken care of?"

"Oh, yeah. She told me about that a week ago and I forgot until she mentioned it last night. Sorry about the short notice."

"No problem. I wanted to talk to you about making up that hour."

"I'm planning to stay late tonight to make it up. I thought I mentioned that in the e-mail."

Holly looked at him and spoke evenly. "You did. I just wanted to let you know that the hour isn't important to me. You committed to getting about forty hours of work done per week. Sometimes that takes you more than forty hours, sometimes less. I'm not worried about you putting the forty hours of time in. I want forty hours' worth of productivity."

"So you don't want me to make up the hour?" Grant said with a confused look.

Holly paused to formulate the right words. "Only if you need to. What I'm interested in is that you get your work done. If you were to finish everything in thirty hours, I'd expect you to see if others needed help. We'd also have a conversation about whether your estimates are accurate. But if you get all of your tasks done for the week, I don't see a reason for you to make up the hour just for the sake of being here."

"I understand," Grant said. "It's just that the last project I worked on, Pete tracked every hour I worked. Come to think of it, he was more interested in the number of hours I worked than what I got done."

"It's not all that uncommon," Holly said. "I'd just rather measure performance rather than hours."

Grant seemed to understand and thanked her. Holly walked away shaking her head thinking about how the practices of other project managers were influencing her team's behavior.

As Holly turned to make her way up to the DBA's office, Emily approached her. "I have something I need to talk to you about," Emily asked her.

"Can you walk and talk?" Holly asked.

Emily walked with Holly to the elevators and explained an issue she was having trying to get the user group from accounting to coordinate their schedules for a business requirements review session. When the doors opened on the eighth floor, she followed Holly to Danielle's office and watched Holly tap on the door.

"Hi, Holly, what's up?" Danielle said.

"How are you today, Danielle?"

"Doing well, but busy," Danielle answered.

"I wanted to check in on a request Eric made last week to allow him and Dominic access to the customer database," Holly said. "Eric said he submitted it a week ago."

Danielle started tapping on her laptop. After a few seconds she said, "Oh, I see it here. Looks like they need management authorization."

"Who are we waiting for to authorize it?"

"Angela Neilson is usually the one we have sign for that database."

Holly crinkled her nose. "Angela is out on maternity leave. Has that request been sitting on her desk for a week?"

"That's entirely possible," Danielle said without any trace of concern in her voice.

"Does she have someone covering for her?" Holly asked, starting to show her annoyance.

"Probably. I'll check into it and --"

"That's okay," Holly cut her off. "I'll do it."

Holly headed to Angela's office with Emily tagging along close behind. In a matter of minutes, Holly found the form sitting on Angela's desk, along with a handful of other forms. "How long do you think that would have sat on Angela's desk?" Holly asked.

"Who knows?" Emily said with a critical look on her face.

Holly grabbed all of the papers and called the HR office from Angela's phone. "Yes, I need a signature from Angela Neilson, but she's out on maternity leave. Can you tell me who is covering for her while she's out?"

After a moment's delay, they gave her a name and Holly thanked them. Holly took all of the forms to an office two doors down and introduced herself to Mitch Long. After explaining the situation with Danielle and Angela and her need for a signature, Mitch promised to sign the form by lunch time.

"Can I stop by at 1:30 and pick it up?" Holly asked.

"Sure," Mitch replied.

As they headed back downstairs on the elevator, Holly asked Emily which members of the accounting team she was having trouble with. Emily gave her three names.

"The usual suspects," Holly replied.

"They seem to have meetings nine hours a day," replied Emily.

"I'll talk to them and make sure they prioritize these meetings," Holly said

When Holly returned to her floor, she walked over to Brandon's desk and asked to speak with him. As they sat down in an empty conference room, Holly gave him a reassuring smile and asked, "How are things going?"

Brandon was surprised to be called aside in the first place and raised his eyebrows a bit defensively. Their one-on-one wasn't scheduled for another three days.

"Uh...okay, I guess," he said. "Why do you ask?"

"You've seemed a bit quiet lately and I wanted to know if everything was okay," Holly said.

155

Brandon paused for a moment and considered pretending nothing was wrong. But then decided to confide in Holly. "I'm a little concerned about the discussions you've been having regarding the next phase of the project."

Holly was surprised to hear that he was even aware that the next phase was being discussed. She had held some initial conversations with Sam and some of the other executives, but no one else had been involved. "What discussions are you talking about?"

"I've heard that I won't be on the project."

The look of astonishment showed on Holly's face. The preliminary conversations hadn't even determined what functionality would be included, let alone how the team would be staffed. "Where did you hear that?"

Brandon looked a little sheepishly at Holly and said, "Rumors have been flying around all over."

"Let me make this clear," said Holly. "We haven't even figured out the scope of the next phase. That won't be done for at least another month. And staffing won't be discussed until the scope has been completely nailed down. I have no plans to remove you from the project or to keep you off of the next phase. It hasn't even been decided whether I'll be on it, let alone any other staffing decisions. Do you have any idea where these rumors started?"

"No," said Brandon. "I just heard that they were going to cut back on developers."

"If you hear anything like that again, tell them what I just told you. But more importantly, if you start to hear rumors, let me know. Don't just sulk or jump to conclusions based on them," she replied emphatically.

Brandon was a little embarrassed, but more grateful that Holly sat down and spoke with him. He had been preoccupied with these thoughts for three days for no reason. Her observance and frankness made him feel much better.

Later that afternoon, Emily saw Holly in the hallway, holding a grocery bag in one hand and a piece of paper in the other. Holly smiled at Emily. "I hold here the database access authorization."

"Sweet," Emily replied with a smile.

"I also talked to the folks in accounting," said Holly. "They rearranged their schedules and made themselves free Thursday afternoon. You can book it for two o'clock."

"You know how to get things done," Emily said with a smile.

"That's just part of my job," Holly replied.

"Thanks, Holly," Emily said. "What's in the bag?"

"Follow me," Holly said as she led Emily to the team room.

Eric and Brandon sat among the other developers in the room discussing the coding approach for a new module when they saw Holly walk in with the grocery bag.

She set the bag on the table and pulled out two half gallons of ice cream, one chocolate and one vanilla, along with some plastic bowls and spoons. "It has come to my attention that Brett just had his article on stored procedures published in *Tech Journal Online*," Holly announced.

The room broke out in applause. Most of them knew about the article, but a few were surprised. "To commemorate this occasion," Holly continued, "we are having a mini-ice cream social. Who wants chocolate and who wants vanilla?"

The team gathered around as Holly filled the bowls with ice cream. As Brett grabbed his bowl he turned to Holly. "Thanks for doing this Holly," he said. "I really appreciate it."

"You guys work really hard and you've been putting in some long hours," said Holly. "I think it's important to make sure we recognize personal and team achievements like this."

"We appreciate it," Eric said. "You do a good job of bringing in doughnuts for birthdays and taking the team out for special lunches when we finish a big job. That makes a big difference."

Holly smiled and said, "All work and no play, you know."

"You also do a good job of keeping things light even in our daily meetings. You joke around and make sure it's fun on a regular basis," Brandon added.

"Just because this is the biggest, most important project in the company's history doesn't mean we can't have a little fun," Holly replied. "You should be having fun on a daily basis. Otherwise you're going to get stressed out. That's when you start making big mistakes or calling in sick as a result of the stress."

They all agreed that even though they were working harder than they had on any other project, that they were also having fun.

"I like coming in to work every day," Eric said. "Besides, I eat better here than I would if I were at home."

Lessons Learned

Tip #61 – Measure performance, not hours

A good project manager knows that just because team members are recording hours, they aren't necessarily being productive. Focusing on timely completion of tasks instead of hours served is the best way to verify that progress is being made on the project.

Tip #62 – Remove obstacles

One of the most important duties of a project manager is to remove obstacles that the members of the team face. Project team members are busy working on their assigned tasks and don't have the time or the access to people in other departments to obtain approvals or request outside work to be completed.

Holly knew that by talking directly with the database manager and the accounting team members, she could remove obstacles for her team members and get them back on track to productivity.

Tip #63 – Be observant for what is not there

Most team members will provide facts and answer questions when they're asked. Some are uncomfortable confronting their manager about issues they are having or about rumors they've heard. An observant project manager should listen for what the team member is not saying.

The team member may be holding back on some silent fears or hiding critical information about the project status. In the latter case, the project manager should dig deep enough to make sure she knows each team member's specific status.

Tip #64 – Make it fun for the team

Most projects are run at full capacity with little slack time built in. Whatever spare time is provided is usually consumed by changes and overruns. This can create a hectic and stressful schedule throughout the project.

Taking time to thank the team, recognize an accomplishment or a milestone, and just having some fun with them on a day-to-day basis can make a big improvement to morale and productivity.

Chapter 18 – Leading without Authority

The elevator doors opened to reveal the smiling, if not acidic, face of Pete. What a way to start the day, thought Holly, trying hard to hide her irritation.

"Just the person I've been looking for," Pete said in his standard cocksure attitude. "Where have you been?"

"In my car driving to work," Holly said, walking past him indifferently.

"You have a real problem on your hands today," he said, following her through the double-glass doors that led to their third-floor office space.

"I have problems on my hands every day. It's my job to solve problems." Holly wasn't about to let Pete get to her that easily.

"Emily and Brett just had it out in the conference room. She was yelling at him about not following the business rules in his code. He shot back that she wrote crappy business rules that were impossible to follow."

"Thanks," she said, closing her office door before he could ruin her day any further.

She sat down and turned on her laptop. There was no e-mail from either Brett or Emily. She decided to wait it out and see if they came to her. Besides, she would see them in the stand-up meeting in fifteen minutes.

The stand-up meeting started like most others. Holly selected someone to start and they went around the room. When it came around to Grant, he mentioned that he was behind on his current task, but promised that he could get it done by Friday.

"Are you comfortable that you know the details well enough to commit to that?" Holly asked.

"Yes," Grant responded confidently. "I feel good about this. I can get it done by Friday."

Next up in the meeting was Brandon. He reported that he had not completed his task that was due the previous Friday because his boss, Steve, had asked him to work on some other items.

Holly knew that Brandon was dedicated ninety percent to the project to allow him to work on occasional tasks outside of the project. This task pulled him away for the full day on Friday, which caused him to miss his deadline.

She was tempted to reprimand Brandon for not getting his task completed, but she thought better of it. She knew that although Brandon was assigned to her project, he technically reported to Steve and that he would prioritize the assignments he gets from Steve. She decided she would speak with Steve later.

As the meeting came to a close, Holly noticed that neither Emily nor Brett said anything about their disagreement and neither one approached Holly to help them resolve it.

After the meeting Emily followed Holly back to her desk. "So will you be checking in on Grant throughout the week on his promise to get his task done by Friday?" Emily asked.

Holly shook her head. "Aside from getting his update in the daily standup? No, I consider that micromanagement. He committed to Friday and I'm going to trust him until he gives me a reason not to."

"What if Friday comes and he doesn't have it done?" Emily asked.

"Then he will have betrayed a minor trust. After that, I'll probably manage him a little closer for other tasks. But I need him to trust me, too. If I micromanage him like that, he's not going to trust me."

Emily wasn't convinced. "What if he continues to betray your trust after that? Do you start managing him closer and closer?"

"If he does it again," Holly said, "we'll have a talk. But if it occurs more often beyond that, I'll do what I need to do to get him off of the project. I just don't have the time or the interest in working that hard at managing anyone. Think of it this way. If he continues to betray my trust over and over, I'm not going to trust him to have any responsibility in the future. If I'm on him all the time, he'll know I don't trust him and he's not going to trust me. It becomes a downward spiral. I have to be able to trust every person on my team and I need them to trust me. If I start out not trusting them, they'll never trust me."

Emily thought about it for a minute. "Most of the managers I've had have done it exactly the opposite. They start out by watching my every move until they develop more trust in me."

"Me too," Holly said. "I've found that when they start with mistrust, it takes a lot longer to develop trust. I've never gotten burned by an employee and I've always been able to develop strong trusting relationships from the start."

That afternoon, Holly found her way over to Steve's office. "Hey Steve, do you have a minute?"

"Sure, Holly," said Steve. "Come on in."

Holly sat down and they exchanged small talk. Finally, Steve asked, "So what can I do for you?"

Holly paused momentarily. "Brandon mentioned in our stand-up meeting today that he did some work for you on Friday."

163

"Yes," Steve replied. "We had a production issue and I needed him to handle an issue related to some code he had written. I was under the impression we were allowed to pull him from time to time."

"Certainly, we built in some time for those types of occurrences," Holly said. "I was wondering, when those situations occur, if you would mind letting me know you're pulling him. It's not that big of a deal if you pull him, but I'd like to know so I can reassign his tasks to someone else if I need to."

"Sure. I'm sorry. I should have thought of that," Steve said apologetically.

"It's not a big deal," Holly said. "It just helps me be a little more proactive."

"I definitely understand, Holly. Thanks for letting me know," Steve said.

Holly looked at the time on her phone and said, "Sorry, Steve, I have to run to a meeting. I'll talk to you later."

Holly ran down the hallway to the conference room to find Eric settling into one of the ergonomic chairs in the conference room. Eric had come to view these one-on-one meetings he had with Holly every other week as a formality and something of a waste of time. She would ask him how things are going and how the project fits into his goals. He would reply that it's going well and that he's satisfied with his career. He didn't feel much was learned by either of them, and he had a lot of work to do.

"So…is the project going well for you?" Holly asked.

Eric smiled to himself at the predictability and said, "Yeah, it's going great."

"That's good to hear. How about the team? Do you get along with everyone alright?"

Eric thought about the question for a second. "Uh, sure… there are people I like more than others, but I get along with everyone on the team. Why do you ask?"

"Well, it's something that I'm concerned about with everyone," Holly said. "I want to make sure there's no conflict. I've also noticed that when you finish pieces of your work, you don't always let the appropriate people know. There could be any number of reasons for that. Maybe you just don't think about it. But I want to make sure it's not an interpersonal issue."

"When have I not let people know?" Eric asked.

"The first time I noticed it was when you finished your piece of the sales module a few weeks ago," Holly said. "You finished the coding piece and the testing team needed to know so they could begin integration testing it with the other modules. It sat for two days before they were aware."

"I just didn't think to let them know," Eric said a little defensively.

"That's what I assumed at the time," Holly said, trying to be agreeable. "But then Monday, you figured out a new approach to calculating delivery charges for items coming from multiple sources. That would have been valuable information for the order entry development team."

"Again, I just didn't think about their need to know," said Eric.

"I understand that," Holly said. "I just want to understand if there's actually more to it. If there are people on the team that you don't get along with, it's something we need to deal with. Not thinking about the next level is a smaller, but different problem. I'd like to have you start thinking about the dependencies of your work. Who needs to know and how to make sure you're keeping people up to date. You're working on the new inventory control module right?"

"Yes, I'll be on that through the end of the week," Eric replied.

"When you're done with that, who needs to have it next?" asked Holly.

165

"Probably the testing team," answered Eric. "I'll make sure to let them know when I'm done."

"That's great," said Holly. "Also, if you think you'll be done earlier or later, make sure to think about who needs to know that and make sure you let them know as far in advance as possible. This is something I'd like you to work on for the rest of the project. Making sure to think about who needs to know your status and keeping them up to date."

Eric looked a little confused. "So am I in trouble for this?" he asked.

"Not at all," Holly countered. "The whole purpose of these one-on-one meetings is for feedback. I don't want to wait until the project is over and say, 'You did a bad job of communicating your status in your project review.' I'd rather let you know about things as I notice them. That will give you a chance to improve on it. Then in your project review, I can mention how well you did improving on that."

"That makes sense," Eric said thoughtfully.

"I expect the same back from you," said Holly. "If you see anything that I'm doing where I need to improve or if I'm not removing obstacles that need to be addressed, I expect you to tell me. I'm not perfect and I'd rather you point those things out to me rather than complaining to your peers about it. I want you to know that I'm always open to your feedback."

Eric's heartbeat was slowing back down to its normal speed. "That's good to know. I can't think of anything right now, but if I do I'll be sure to let you know."

As they ended their one-on-one session, Eric asked Holly, "Do you do these one-on-one sessions with every person on the team?"

"Yes," answered Holly. "I meet with each team member every two weeks for fifteen minutes."

"That seems like a big time commitment. Do you feel like you accomplish a lot in these sessions?"

Holly smiled. "We accomplish more than you realize. Maybe we don't make a lot of decisions or chart our next direction like we do in other meetings. But it forces us to sit down and just talk about how you're doing, if you have any problems, and how this project is contributing to your career goals. Also, if I have a problem with your performance, it allows us to talk about it without scheduling a special meeting for it. I can make it less of a big deal by just bringing it up here."

"You mean like me not communicating?" Eric smiled.

Holly laughed. "Eric, you're one of the best on the team. But seriously, our one-on-one meetings give me great insight, from you and everyone else on the project, on how the project meets your career goals. I report that back to Sam in my one-on-one with him. That gives him input on staffing for future projects."

"I didn't realize you put that much thought into it," said Eric. "And I didn't realize you were that interested. I just figured you managed everyone's tasks and watched the budget."

"That's the management part of my job, and I can't take my eye off the ball on that aspect. But part of my job is to be a leader. Making sure the team is happy, that everyone feels like they're making a difference, and making sure their career has meaning is just as important."

Eric looked at her thoughtfully, "I didn't realize there was that much to it. I just figured we were chatting."

"There's also a leadership aspect to getting the tasks done," said Holly. "It's not just a matter of comparing the date someone gets a task done to its due date. I need to make sure I'm motivating the team members. If all I did was drive you hard to get things done on time, you would start to lose your motivation. That's why we do team lunches where I stand up and thank everyone for their efforts."

"That makes sense," said Eric.

As he walked out of the conference room, Eric felt he had made a transformation. He walked in thinking the meeting was a waste of time. He now realized that Holly was on his side trying to improve his performance and make sure he got a good evaluation in his final review.

Back at her desk, Holly was happy to see that there was another lunch-and-learn session being presented by Paul today. One of the cultural norms that she had noticed with both of the combined companies was the belief that knowledge is power. Each person on the team, regardless of which organization they were from, was hesitant to share any specialized knowledge they had of their system or of any technological specialty they had.

This was particularly frustrating for Holly because each team member had some form of specialized knowledge of their own company's system and the technology it was written in. This required business analysts, programmers, architects, database administrators, and analysts from both companies.

She had specialized knowledge herself on Harrison's applications and several weeks ago she had decided to do something about it. She scheduled a lunch-and-learn session in which she presented an overview of Harrison's applications. She showed a high level flow of how the whole system worked and then began drilling into each of the components. She described the purpose of each element and any special processing that wasn't intuitive. Holly described how data flowed to and from each system and handed out a schema of the database with all of the other documentation for everyone on the team for future reference.

She decided to get the rest of the team involved. In a one-on-one meeting with Dominic she asked him, "What did you think of the lunch and learn I did last week?"

"I thought it was very informative. I knew a lot of it, but I could tell that some of the folks from Lee were pretty enlightened," Dominic said.

"Thanks," said Holly. "As a database developer from the Harrison side, I was wondering if you would be willing to hold a similar session to give an overview of the database for the technical team."

"I don't know," Dominic responded. "I'm not very good at presenting."

"It's not a formal speech, Dominic," Holly insisted. "These are people you work with every day. You're just talking about something that you know well. There's nothing to be afraid of."

Dominic reluctantly agreed.

A few days later, Dominic presented his database overview. After his presentation, Danielle, a database administrator from Lee Foods, came up to Holly and told her how helpful these sessions have been. "I learned a lot about your system and the database that I couldn't have learned from just reading the documentation."

"That's great Danielle," said Holly. "How would you like to give an overview of the Lee database next week?"

Danielle froze. "I- I'm not very good at public speaking," she said weakly.

"Tell you what," said Holly. "How about if you and Eric get together and create a presentation? If you provide the information, you and Eric can do a joint presentation so you won't be so nervous."

Lacking another excuse not to, Danielle reluctantly complied. The next week Danielle and Eric presented an overview of the Lee database that prompted so many questions that they went an extra forty minutes. That was fine with Holly. She had finally gotten team members to share information.

She began hitting up the business analysts. They finally got to a point where they were holding at least one and often two lunch-and-learn sessions each week.

Holly began to see two separate teams begin to weave into a single cohesive team. They were enjoying having lunch together and sharing information. As an added bonus, Holly found that team members who were anxious about public speaking were getting some good experience presenting information they were familiar with.

There were still significant gaps in knowledge between the two companies' employees, but they were making progress in sharing information both through the lunch and learns and through their daily interactions.

Holly smiled as she reflected on how the team had evolved from being protective of information to freely sharing it. She grabbed her lunch and headed to the conference room. Walking past the elevators, she saw Sam and Pete apparently leaving for lunch together. Again, the questions ran through Holly's head, wondering what they were discussing. Her concerns caused her to miss most of what Paul said in his session.

After lunch, Holly looked up to see Pete in her office doorway. "What did you do about the Emily and Brett blowup?" he asked.

"Nothing," she replied without looking up.

"What do you mean nothing?"

She raised her head and looked him straight in the eye. "They haven't asked me to do anything. They're mature adults and can handle issues like that on their own. If it begins affecting their productivity, or anyone else's, I'll help moderate them to an agreement. Unless that happens, I trust them to resolve their own problems."

"Suit yourself," he said. "If you ask me, that pot could boil over if you don't remove the flame. That may be why Sam has asked me to be a little more up on things."

170

"More up on things?" Holly asked. "What does that mean?"

"Oh, I don't know," he said, working hard to be nonchalant. "Who knows what he's thinking." Pete left her office, trying his best to leave a mysterious aura.

Holly went back to work trying to forget Pete's existence.

That evening, Holly savored the smell of the chicken sizzling on the grill. She was lost in thought as she sat on Chad's patio watching him stand at the grill.

Chad was suddenly standing over her. "Something on your mind?" he asked.

Holly was startled. "Oh. I was just thinking of something."

"I could tell. I asked you a question twice and you never even heard me. You were a million miles away."

"Sorry," Holly said. "Something's been bothering me at work."

"What's up this time?" he asked.

"Oh, nothing. I don't want to bother you with it."

"You're not bothering me. And besides, you'll be lost in thought for the rest of the evening if you don't talk this out."

Holly smiled a grateful smile at her understanding boyfriend. "I keep seeing Pete and Sam together and it's just got me a little disturbed." She told Chad about the conversation she had with Pete that afternoon. "I've had a few slip-ups on the project and I'm just concerned that Sam is thinking about replacing me with Pete. I've spent the last two nights updating my résumé."

Chad turned the chicken breasts over on the grill. "Have you talked to Sam about this at all?"

"No, it's all been speculation on my part up until now," said Holly.

Chad put some final seasoning on the chicken breasts before taking them off the grill. "Based on what Pete said today, I don't think it's speculation anymore. It can't hurt to at least ask Sam whether he's satisfied with your work or not."

"You're right," said Holly. "I just need to figure out the right way to ask that doesn't sound too pathetic."

"You have a way with words," said Chad. "I'm sure you'll think of something. Now that you've talked it out, are you ready to eat?"

"I'm ready," she said. "That smells terrific."

Lessons Learned

Tip #65 – Resist the urge to manage

Project managers have plenty of issues to resolve in the course of a day. If two people have an issue that doesn't require your involvement, it's sometimes best to stay out of it. It becomes a judgment call determining when and how to get involved.

Interpersonal issues are often best resolved by the people involved. If productivity is not affected for those involved or others around them, spend your energy managing other aspects of the project.

Tip #66 - Know your authority and its limits

By diplomatically speaking with Steve, Holly got her message across to him and made him understand the ramifications his actions had on her project. Her first instinct was to take it out on Brandon. Brandon is in a difficult situation, though. Working in a matrixed organization, he is essentially praising two gods – he reports to Steve but also to Holly on the project.

If Steve habitually pulls team members away to a point where it creates a significant impact on Holly's project, she has the authority to escalate the problem to the executive team. This may be a last resort for Holly. Taking action like that is bound to hurt her relationship with both Steve and Brandon, making them less likely to cooperate in the future.

Tip #67 – Develop trust in both directions

Many managers distrust their employees until given a reason to trust. By trusting them first, team members are more likely to live up to the trust and will trust their manager back.

The alternative is to micromanage employees, which hurts trust and costs both the manager and the employee additional time that could be spent doing more productive tasks.

Tip #68 – Provide regular feedback to team members

Rather than waiting until the end of a project or the team member's service anniversary, the project manager should meet one-on-one with each team member at least every two weeks to get a feel for how they're doing on the project and how the project is helping them with their career goals.

Additionally, if there are improvement opportunities, the project manager should provide feedback early and often. If a team member finds out about a weakness several months after the fact, they have less opportunity to show improvement.

Tip #69 – Be a leader and a manager

A large part of the project manager's responsibility is to develop the professional careers of each team member. The one-on-one meeting, in addition to providing feedback, allows the project manager to mentor the team members and make sure that they are advancing in their careers appropriately. Employees often leave a company for an opportunity that fits their career goals better. The project manager could have provided the employee with similar opportunities, if he or she had taken the time to find out the employees interests.

Tip #70 – Share knowledge and encourage it in the team

It's common in many corporate cultures to hold on to knowledge. Many assume that the more knowledge they hold onto, the more power and control they hold. On a project, it is important for the project manager to create and promote an environment of knowledge sharing to ensure success for the entire project.

Chapter 19 – Taking Issue

Danielle had an ominous look on her face when she walked into the conference room. Holly was already a bit anxious at the fact that Danielle called an emergency meeting. She and Emily just looked at each other when they saw her face.

"I assume you didn't call this meeting to tell me some good news," Holly started out.

"No," said Danielle. "You're correct in that assumption. Do you remember when we talked about performing analysis on the data model a few weeks ago?"

Holly thought for a few seconds and said, "Yeah, we talked about your team being so short-handed. You had a pretty new developer working on it right?"

"Yeah, it was Brent," Danielle said. "He did a pretty good job at first, but he missed several database tables. We need to add them now and it's going to have impact on the development timeline."

"How did he miss something so big?" Emily asked.

"He's new and didn't realize it was in scope for the project."

"Didn't you already have an issue for that Holly?" Emily asked.

"No, but I identified having a newer, inexperienced data analyst as a risk," Holly replied.

"Did you have any mitigation strategies for this risk?' Danielle asked.

"We kind of accepted the risk," said Holly. "We decided that if it happened, we would pull in a consultant to perform analysis. We'll have to bring in a consultant to review the data model and make the updates. Then we'll determine the impact to the project. It's not the best thing to happen, because it will be a hit to the budget and the timeline. But we knew it was a possibility and we have a plan for it now that it's an issue."

Danielle breathed a little easier, seeing that Holly already had a fallback plan for the situation.

As Emily walked down the hall with Holly after the meeting, she asked, "So you're ready for any issue based on the risks you identified?"

"No," Holly replied. "We can't think of every possible situation, but identifying risks lets us consider a big chunk of them. If we're lucky, we consider most of them and have solutions in our back pocket. A lot of issues come up that we never considered as risks. Even then, we might be more prepared if we did the risk analysis. Contingencies for one risk might give us ideas for another issue that comes up."

"So where are you headed to now?" asked Emily.

"I'm going to update the issues list with our new issue," Holly answered. "I also have to arrange for a consultant to come in."

Less than an hour later, Holly was sitting at her desk making updates to her project plan and contemplating how the database developer issue would affect the schedule when Emily darkened her doorway.

"Holly, you aren't going to believe this!"

"What's up?"

Emily sat down across from Holly's desk. "I just got off the phone with Menlo Systems. They were supposed to deliver their data conversion software by next week. They told me that because of a number of different delays, they can't deliver it until the end of next month. This is going to set our project back an entire month. We needed that software to start our data conversion by the first of next month to stay on track. This is just a disaster."

Holly was disappointed. The software delivery by Menlo Systems was a major dependency for her data conversion milestone.

"That is disheartening, isn't it?" she finally said.

"It's more than disheartening. It's a major blow to the project," Emily said.

"Well let's see about that. Let's get the right team members together and discuss what we can do about it. I'll schedule a meeting for this afternoon with Danielle, Dominic, you, and me to discuss the situation and figure out what our options are and what we can do. There's always an answer. We just need to find it."

When Holly walked into the conference room that afternoon, she found Emily sitting with Danielle and Dominic. Emily had already started explaining the issue of Menlo Systems and the delay. She said that she had scheduled a call with Menlo to find out what was behind the delay. Holly was holding out hope that they could work out an agreement with the vendor to try to get the software earlier than they had estimated. But it was important to come up with some options if they indeed had to wait until the end of next month to acquire the software.

Danielle stated that they had done an assessment of data conversion software packages and the package from Menlo Systems had shown advantages over the other packages. The main advantage Menlo had over Claremont, the runner-up package, was that the licensing fees were about $5,000 lower. Claremont also appeared to be more difficult to implement than Menlo's package.

Holly asked Danielle to contact Claremont and determine how soon they'd be able to deliver to see if that was even still an option. "Perhaps we could negotiate a lower licensing fee," she suggested, "or obtain additional budget if we can get their software sooner."

Dominic had a smug look on his face. As the database developer, he had advocated writing the data conversion software themselves instead of buying it. "If you had just allowed me to write the conversion software, we wouldn't be in this mess," he said.

Holly cut him off immediately. "Maybe so, Dominic. But that does nothing to help us now." She remembered his arguments well, but had decided against the proposal, knowing that delays and quality issues were more likely with code written internally than with a software package. She also knew that at this late date, there was no way they could write the software in-house before Menlo could deliver.

"What we need," Emily added, "is ideas to help solve the problem at hand."

Dominic spoke up. "Do we need all of the data converted or just some portion? If we only needed selected data, we could write some simple queries by the beginning of next month to convert that data. That might give us enough data until Menlo can deliver their package."

"That's an interesting thought," said Emily. "We were going to convert by food category for some initial testing. If we could determine which categories would enable the simplest queries, maybe we could just resequence the order of the categories we test. That might allow us to start making progress on the data conversion until Menlo can deliver."

Holly said, "That's a good thought. We weren't scheduled to begin analysis of the Frozen Foods distribution component until later in the project. What if we did that analysis while we waited for the data conversion software? That would free up those BAs to help with data conversion analysis later on."

"That would depend on the availability of my BAs in the next couple of weeks," responded Emily. "I'll check on that to see if it's an option."

They brainstormed a little longer, but it seemed like the three initial ideas were their best options. When the team came to consensus that those were the best three ideas, Holly announced, "Okay, let's look into these options and get together tomorrow to see which is the most feasible. Danielle, let me know what you find out from Claremont and their ability to deliver. In the meantime, I'll look into the flexibility we have in the budget for the more costly software."

"Emily," Holly continued, "can you work with Dominic to determine the least complex food categories for conversion and see what we could get done by the first of next month? Also, check into the availability your BAs have starting next week to see if we can get them going earlier on other tasks. Let's all have a follow-up meeting tomorrow so we can report back what we find out."

The next day when they reconvened, Danielle reported that she had spoken to the sales rep at Claremont Systems. "The news isn't great," Danielle said. "Their implementation team is busy and wouldn't be able to deliver until just a week earlier than Menlo."

"There is additional budget to acquire the Claremont software," replied Holly, "but I don't think it would be worth it to get the functionality only one week sooner than we'll get it from Menlo. I think we're better off waiting the extra week."

Emily was the next to report back. "The BAs that were assigned to do the analysis on the Frozen Foods functionality are tied up on some other work. I do have one that is available. That might help us get enough analysis done up front to free people up for the data analysis later on."

"But working with Dominic," Emily went on, "we determined that if we focused on the Dessert and Beverage

179

categories first, he could develop the queries for those categories within the next two weeks. That would allow us to convert and analyze that data while we wait for the Menlo software to be delivered for the more complex data conversion."

Holly allowed everyone on the team to discuss the pros and cons of this option. Once she felt all of the relevant facts and considerations had been discussed, she said, "It sounds like focusing on Dessert and Beverage categories allows us the most productive option. Dominic, please start working on the queries right now. Emily, can we use your available BA to work with them on the appropriate data analysis?"

"I'm texting him right now," Emily responded.

"Danielle, please send my thanks to the folks at Claremont Systems. We may end up working with them someday in the future."

"Will do," Danielle replied.

Holly was proud of her team for being open minded and finding creative ways to solve the problem. She was also proud of herself for facilitating the resolution rather than forcing her idea onto the team. As it turned out, they came up with the better solution.

As they filed out of the conference room, Holly pulled Danielle aside to get a status on the new database analyst. Danielle had arranged for the new consultant to come in and analyze the data model. She had already performed an impact analysis to come up with the number of hours the changes would take and determined the impact to the project in terms of time and budget cost for Holly's status report to Sam.

The next day as Holly discussed the issue with Sam, he interrupted her. "How did this issue come about?"

"When we put together the staffing model for the project, we were shorthanded on the database team. Danielle didn't have a developer with deep experience in data modeling so we assigned it to Brent."

Sam wrinkled his nose. "Brent's only a few years out of school."

"I know. We just didn't have a lot of choices. Our problem was that we didn't have enough experienced team members to do the job."

Sam shook his head, "Why didn't you look into borrowing Adam? He's assigned to another project right now, but they're on hold because of some vendor issues. He could have spent a few weeks on it and done it right."

"I wasn't aware of his availability," Holly said.

"I'm seeing a couple of problems here," Sam said. "First, we didn't have the right person for the job, so you just assigned whoever you had. Second, it doesn't sound like you looked into all of your options before selecting Brent."

"Those were all of the options we were aware of," Holly said, a little defensively.

"Well, they were the only options you were aware of," said Sam, "but when it wasn't the optimal solution, it would have been nice if you had sought out other options. I'm not trying to be critical. You didn't necessarily do anything wrong. I just want to make sure this is a learning opportunity for you for future situations like this."

Holly nodded in agreement.

Lessons Learned

Tip #71 – Issues are often risks that come true

Because Holly had done detailed risk analysis, she had considered the fact that the database developer was new and inexperienced so she had considered that it could become an issue. When the risk evolved to an issue, she already had a plan for working with an outside consultant to resolve it.

Even if an issue occurs where its risk wasn't considered, doing thorough enough risk analysis will allow faster and easier issue resolution because a risk mitigation strategy for a different risk may provide ideas for resolving other issues.

Tip #72 – Attack every challenge as a problem solver

Major league pitcher Orel Hershiser once spoke of the attitude he used when he went out on the mound to pitch a game. He said that at the beginning of each game, he would go out to the mound expecting to pitch a no-hitter. Whenever he gave up the first hit, he would immediately change his goal to pitch a one-hitter. With each subsequent hit, he changed his goal to do the best he could do moving forward.

He couldn't change what was already done, but he could affect his performance moving forward.

This applies in virtually every aspect of life. When managing a project, things will go wrong. A project manager can complain, find fault, throw a tantrum, or many other things when problems arise. But nothing gets accomplished when that happens.

The best approach is to determine the best way to resolve the issue and move forward.

Tip #73 – Have a method for problem solving

When solving problems, a methodical approach is usually the best. The steps for methodical problem solving are:

- **Clearly define the problem.** In this situation, the problem is that the delay of the software delivery will cause a delay to a critical phase of the project. If Holly and her team focused on the software only, they may have eliminated possible solutions that could just as easily resolve the issue.
- **Solicit input.** Holly asked for input from the team. She also made it clear that they needed to look forward rather than harp on past decisions and how things might have been different.
- **Consider alternative solutions.** Holly allowed everyone to speak and provide ideas. Although she already had an approach in mind, she wanted to get everyone's ideas.
- **Determine pros and cons of each option.** There is usually no perfect solution. Each one is bound to have tradeoffs. By discussing and analyzing the tradeoffs of each idea, the team was able to come to an agreeable solution. It won't always be obvious and sometimes the project manager has to make a difficult decision.
- **Make a decision and develop an action plan.** Once a direction has been determined, create a plan to execute it and move forward.

Tip #74 – Determine the root cause

Holly and Danielle had determined that the problem they were solving was that the person they assigned to the job was inexperienced. Sam opened Holly's perspective by explaining that Brent wasn't the problem. The issue was that they did not consider all of their options for staffing the position.

Chapter 20 – Scoping It Out

The e-mail came just as Holly was getting ready to shut her laptop down for the night. She heard the beep indicating its arrival and had that split-second conversation in her head. Should I, or shouldn't I? She decided to read it and not leave it for the morning.

Dominic was asking Grant a question about how the data would be used for his application. As Holly had requested, she was copied on all of these e-mails. She didn't always understand all of the technical detail, but she wanted to stay informed on the technical conversations.

Dominic's question referred to a new column on the main web page that Grant was developing. She read through it quickly and then powered down her laptop. As she drove home, her mind wandered, thinking about what she had accomplished for the day. After a few minutes, she thought about Dominic's e-mail. She couldn't remember discussing the new column he was asking about.

When she got home, she powered her laptop back up and read the e-mail again. Then she pulled up the business requirements document and reread the section that related to the page Grant was developing. There was no mention of the column and it did not show in the screen prototype. She responded to Dominic's e-mail, copying Grant and Emily.

> Dominic:
>
> When did this column get added to this page? I don't see it in the business requirements document and

don't remember discussing it during the design sessions.

Holly

The question was directed more toward Emily as the business analyst than either Dominic or Grant.

The next morning, Holly hadn't even taken her laptop out of her bag before Emily was at her door. She was not surprised since Emily was usually in earlier than everyone.

"Hey, I saw your e-mail about the new column on Grant's page. I had been meaning to talk to you about that," Emily said.

"What's it about?" Holly asked.

"It came up in a meeting with the users two days ago. I just hadn't had a chance to discuss it."

Holly paused and chose her words carefully. "I understand how busy everyone is but we can't add functionality just because the users ask for it. We need to get approval for each change. Otherwise it gets out of control."

"That's true, but they said it needed to be done and approval would have taken a week. We need to have this application done by Friday to meet our deadline," said Emily.

"We can't fall to that pressure," replied Holly. "We need to monitor for any change and make sure we get appropriate approval before doing it. If it pushes the schedule out, that's what the impact of the change is. They need to decide whether the change is worth the delay. If we try to squeeze functionality in an already tight schedule, we run behind without any approval from the client. Then they blame us for being late." Holly decided to stop before it became a rant. She wondered if she was too late for that.

"It just seemed like a simple change," said Emily.

"It had a database change and a new column on a screen that needs to go through several approvals. How could that be simple?" Holly responded, realizing that she was now officially ranting.

Emily paused, realizing the significance of the change. "What do we do now?"

"I'll write up a change request for the user team to approve. If we can get it through by the end of the day tomorrow, we'll be alright. If they delay, I won't guarantee them anything. In the meantime, we need to stop Dominic and Grant from doing anything else before we get approval."

"I'll let them know. Do you need any help with the change request?"

"No," Holly said. "I can take care of that, thanks."

Emily left to notify the developers while Holly sat down at her desk, glad that she had checked last night's e-mail before she left.

In less than an hour, Holly had completed the change request form. She also added it to the change control log spreadsheet she had created at the beginning of the project.

Once she proofread the request, she was ready to send it out to the team. The change request form included information such as the names of the project sponsors, the type of change, and at which phase of the project the request was made. It then provided larger sections for Holly to describe the change, explain how it impacted the project from a timeline and budget perspective, and an approval section for the project sponsor to sign off. The person that requested the change also had an area to approve the change.

Holly e-mailed the change request to Grant, Dominic, and the quality assurance lead. She asked them to meet with her first thing the next morning so they could each provide the impact the change would have on the project.

The next morning, Holly sat down with the group. They each discussed the impact the change had on their area. The combined impact was not large and Holly and the rest of the team members believed they could absorb the change without affecting the timeline or the budget of the project.

As Holly started to close the meeting, Emily spoke up. "I don't know if this is the right time to bring this up, but there are three other minor changes that have occurred over the past few weeks." She pulled up a document on her laptop and displayed it on the wall through the projector.

Holly looked at the changes. "I've got each of these documented in the change log."

"Are you going to write up a change request for each of these?" Emily asked.

"No. I've actually been accumulating them. I'll include them in this change request just to make the business team aware of all of the work that we're absorbing. I prefer combining small changes like that rather than sending them a full document every time there is a change."

Holly updated the change request with the findings of the meeting and the additional changes and sent it to the users and the project sponsor. She would require their approval before the developers could start implementing the change.

With all that accomplished, Holly was glad to get out of the office. She had a one-on-one lunch appointment with Sam.

Holly smiled as the waiter refilled her raspberry tea. There were many reasons that she enjoyed her biweekly lunches with Sam, not the least of which was that she got to dine at restaurants like Cocina de Pablo, an upscale Spanish-themed restaurant.

She also liked the fact that Sam took her away from the office every two weeks to see how she was doing, give her a pep talk if necessary, and provide her with advice from his years of experience. Sam treated it as more of a mentoring session than a status meeting and Holly liked that.

"How do you feel the Merge-Tech project is going?" Sam asked.

"Well there's probably nothing I could say that would make you more nervous than if I told you things were perfect," Holly joked.

"You're right about that," he said with a smile.

"There are a few nagging issues that I'm dealing with but we are pretty much on schedule," Holly said. "The developers have been working a little overtime, nothing to burn themselves out yet, but it's allowing them to stay on schedule. No major issues at this point."

"That's great," said Sam. "Sounds like you've got the schedule under control. Not that I want to get into the details, but what are some of the nagging issues you're dealing with?"

"Mostly just small fires I've been putting out. I wasn't aware that they had upgraded the .NET development framework a few weeks ago. That set the developers back a few days while they scrambled to adjust their code set to the new framework."

"I didn't see a change request for that," Sam responded.

"I didn't write one," said Holly. "It wasn't a change in functionality for the project."

"It doesn't have to be a change in business requirements or functionality," Sam replied. "Anything that causes work that you didn't plan on, regardless of whether it affects the schedule, should have a change request written up for it. It protects you down the road if that change ends up costing the project more in time or budget."

"I thought change requests were created just for functionality changes," said Holly.

"New requirements are the most common source of change requests," Sam said, "but they can also be due to changes in technology like that upgrade. I've written change requests for changes in staffing, whether there was a change from the business team or an unplanned new developer added to the project. If there are cost increases for any software or consulting fees, those should get a CR too."

"I hadn't even thought of those," Holly said, trying to think if any of those events had occurred on her project.

"If the developers take any extra time to meet their estimates, have you considered whether they've been gold plating, making things a little more fancy than planned? That ends up costing you time in the development and the testing process. It can be an even bigger problem if they add little niceties and the users don't like it. You end up losing the time they spend doing it as well as the time they spend undoing it. I once had a project where the users added an additional review process with their vice president. Not only did it cost me the extra time for the review, it took me a week and a half just to get on her calendar."

Holly sat there thoughtfully for a few seconds. "The business users just asked me for another review step for their external call center," she said.

"You should write a change request for that," replied Sam. "Even if it doesn't increase the project timeline, every stakeholder should know what changed from the original scope of the project. If nothing else, it opens their eyes to every change you had to deal with. It also gives you some leverage when they ask for a change that does change the timeline. You can show them all of the changes you've already had to manage."

Holly looked at Sam's face. He had a natural sternness about him that made it difficult to tell if he was reprimanding her or just informing her.

The confusion must have shown on her face. Sam looked at her and said "Is there something bothering you, Holly?"

Holly wanted to cry but she was too strong for that. Her voice quivered a bit and a tear welled up in one of her eyes. She gained her composure and her courage back enough to say, "Sam, there has been something bothering me. Are you planning to replace me on this project with Pete?"

"Replace you with Pete?" Sam asked with surprise. "What led you to that belief?"

"I've just seen some writing on the wall. I've had a number of missteps on the project and Pete's project is coming to an end soon. And then Pete indicated that you wanted him to be a little more up on what's going on with my project."

"Wait," Sam said, putting his hand up. "What did Pete say?"

Holly told Sam about the conversations she had with Pete recently.

Sam wrinkled his brow and said, "First of all, let me state emphatically that I have no intention of replacing you with Pete or anyone else. You're doing a fantastic job, Holly. Part of my job is to mentor you. And I'll continue to help you improve. It's not an indicator of dissatisfaction. These missteps you talked about are things I almost expect someone at your level to do. You're doing great, but you're still learning. You're supposed to make mistakes."

Holly breathed a sigh of relief a little louder than she had intended.

"Second," Sam continued, "don't let Pete get to you. I'll deal with him. In the meantime, I would appreciate if you didn't say anything to him about this conversation."

"Okay," Holly said. Sam changed the subject and they didn't discuss the matter any further. Sam's reassurances made her feel better, but she knew she was going to need more than that to regain her full confidence.

Lessons Learned

Tip #75 – Always monitor scope

For many project managers, scope is defined at the beginning of the project. After the initial definition, they tend to take their eye off the ball. Scope begins expanding and they lose control of it, constantly trying to stuff more work into a finite schedule. As the project advances, they realize too late that there is not enough time to do everything they have agreed upon.

A good project manager has her eye open at all times for new changes that may affect the team's ability to get their work done by the scheduled deadline. It is critical to make sure the team doesn't agree to changes requested – or demanded – by the business users. Business users can be strong and make a great case for why functionality is critical for them to do their jobs. But if it was not defined as the original scope for the project, it must be managed as a change in scope.

Tip #76 – Manage scope formally with change controls

When new scope is identified, the project manager should formalize the process by completing a change request form. This form should provide details of the change with its effect on the project including the impact it will have for the team's work effort.

The project manager can then provide the impact of the change to the project to the business team. That will give them the appropriate information to make an informed decision to exclude the change, include it by removing other scope, or increase project resources.

Tip #77 – Avoid "nickel and diming" the customer on scope changes

Many changes will have little or no impact on the project. When small changes occur, the project manager should log them but hold off on creating a change control. Submitting a change control for every small change not only creates a lot of overhead work, but also makes the business owners feel that they are being "nickel and dimed" – charged for every minor modification they request.

The better approach is to accumulate the small changes. When a significant change comes about that warrants a formal change request, include all of the small changes to show the business users the number of changes the team absorbed. This allows the project manager to inform the users of all of the changes while creating some goodwill for the relationship.

Tip #78 – Be aware of hidden scope increases

Not all changes are a matter of the business community asking for new functionality. Changes occur on a regular basis that have nothing to do with business requirements. The technical team can cause their own changes by adding or subtracting a staff member or making technical changes that cause extra work for the team.

Any change that affects – or has potential to impact – the budgeted hours or funding of the project should be logged in the formal change register.

Tip #79 – Confront issues and concerns

Rather than let her concern fester, Holly came out and asked Sam what was going on. Sam could tell that something was bothering her. She laid her cards on the table and told

Sam what was upsetting her. Holly risked hearing what she did not want to hear. But by confronting Sam, she addressed the issue and got the answer to her question.

Chapter 21 – The Confidence of Holly

As soon as she stuck her head into Emily's cubicle, she regretted it. She tried not to show her disappointment, but wasn't sure if she was successful.

"Oh, hi, Pete. I didn't mean to interrupt," Holly said.

"That's okay," Pete said in his cocky way. "Were you looking for me or Emily?"

Well you of course. I always come looking for you in Emily's cubicle, Holly thought. "I have a question for Emily, but I'll stop back later."

"Oh, go ahead. I'm sure what you have to say is more important than my conversation," Pete said.

"Me too, but I'll come back," Holly said.

"By all means, go ahead," Pete said

Holly knew that Pete's insistence was based more on snooping than on being polite. She decided she didn't have anything to hide from him. "Emily, did you send out the requirements document to the business user team?"

"Not yet, you asked me to send it to you for review. I e-mailed it to you yesterday afternoon."

"I forgot that I asked to review them and I won't have time for it until tomorrow. I'd like to get those requirements in front of them right away. Go ahead and send them out. I'll take a look, but I'm sure they're okay."

"I'll send them out right now," Emily replied.

Holly was back in her office for only a few minutes when she saw Pete's smirking face in the doorway. "Way to screw up with Emily," he said.

"What do you mean?" she asked, trying hard to hide her exasperation.

"Let me give you some advice," he said, taking an uninvited seat. "You should review every document that goes out to the users. You never know what kind of crap your team can send out. Second, if you forgot what you told your team, don't admit it to them. That's a perfect recipe to lose credibility."

For an instant, Holly wanted to go across the desk at Pete and punch him in the throat. Instead, she paused for a few seconds and took a deep breath. "I review a lot of the documents that go to the users. I know Emily's work. She's one of the best I've seen. I'm very comfortable with her submitting the document directly to the users. I was only going to review it if I had time. I felt it was more important to get it to the users than to be a bottleneck with my review."

She continued, "I also disagree with you on the credibility issue. I have no problem admitting to a mistake. You'll lose more credibility covering up your mistakes and taking yourself too seriously. Admitting your mistakes will actually build legitimacy with the team."

"How do you figure?" he asked, laughing with exaggerated disbelief.

"If you're wrong about something, they know it whether you admit it or not," Holly said. "If you deny it, they can see through the lie. They'll eventually start questioning everything you say because they don't know what to believe."

Pete stood up, shaking his head. "You can believe that if you want, but if you keep admitting your screw-ups that's what they'll begin seeing you as, a big screw up."

"Thanks," said Holly. "I'll keep that in mind." She knew in her own mind that this wasn't an opinion she shared with Pete.

Pete walked away but Holly sat there wondering. Despite Sam's assurances, Pete still managed to get under her skin. Sam assured her that he wasn't planning to replace her, but why did he not want her to discuss their conversation? What was Sam trying to hide?

Chad came over to Holly's apartment for dinner that night. She shared her conversation with Sam as well as her lingering concerns.

"If Sam was really considering replacing you, he wouldn't have been so reassuring," Chad insisted.

"You're probably right," she said. "I just got a bad vibe when he told me not to talk to Pete about it."

Chad put his arm around Holly. "Go into work with confidence tomorrow, and the next day, and the day after that. If you do that, you're going to be fine."

Holly thought about Chad's words. He was the only person she knew that she could talk to without strain or effort. She smiled at him. "Thanks, Chad. You always know how to make me feel better."

Lessons Learned

Tip #80 – Develop legitimacy with your team

Many managers believe that if they portray an image of infallibility, never admitting to mistakes, that their staff and those around them will believe it.

The contradiction is that by leading with humility and admitting when you are wrong, your team will view you as more legitimate than if you put on a ruse of perfection.

Tip #81 – Manage with confidence

If a project manager receives criticism from peers, she can accept that criticism without second guessing herself. Despite how much Pete annoyed Holly, she approached him confidently when she disagreed with his opinions.

Tip #82 – Trust your instincts

As a project manager, people will tell you that you are wrong and provide unsolicited advice. The best advice is to listen politely and trust your own instincts. If you feel the advisor is right, it's perfectly fine to change your mind. But remember that all advice is optional.

Tip #83 – Control your emotions.

Ask yourself if you are as angry as you feel. Don't blow up in stressful situations. There will be times when people say things to deliberately provoke you and other times when they do it unintentionally. No matter the situation, take a deep breath and allow the moment to pass. Losing your temper will more than likely escalate the problem and make it worse.

Chapter 22 –Mentoring To and From

Holly sat at her desk as if she were an air traffic controller at the control panel. She checked the latest updates on software defect fixes, checked her e-mail, and reviewed her task list for the day. It's going to be another long day, she told herself. Her first task was a two-hour requirements meeting. With her day planned, she smiled defiantly and headed to her first meeting.

She looked down the conference room table listening to Emily explain the next iteration's business rules to the business users. Before long she noticed Dominic and Eric using their mobile devices. Holly made a mental note to talk to them separately about it.

As the meeting went on, she noticed they were smiling and making eye contact. She quickly realized that they were texting each other. She could also tell that almost everyone in the meeting knew they were doing it.

Emily came to the end of a section of the business rules and was preparing to launch into the next section when Holly broke in. "Should we take a five-minute break?"

Everyone nodded and they agreed to reconvene in a five minutes.

Holly met Dominic and Eric at the door and asked to see them in the empty conference room next door. She closed the door and turned toward them. "It's not my management style to call people out on the carpet in front of others so I didn't say anything during the meeting, but did you remember that one of our team norms is to limit electronic usage during meetings?"

Eric spoke up first. "I was actually looking up some documents that were pertinent to the discussion."

"They must have been humorous documents and you must have both been accessing the same ones," Holly said, "because you were both smirking at the same time."

Dominic and Eric made eye contact and knew they were busted. They knew better than to prolong their fabricated defense.

"Guys," she continued, "I know that not all of the business requirements Emily is going over apply to everyone in the meeting. But I need everyone to be engaged and we can't have this electronic note passing. It's distracting and I'm sure I'm not the only one that saw what was going on. You're not as subtle as you think you are."

They both nodded and walked through the door she held open for them. She glanced at each of them on occasion over the rest of the morning. They were model citizens. Although no one heard what she said to them, she knew that most of the team saw her pull them aside and noticed that the texting had stopped. She was glad she stopped them when she did. She also hoped that it would set an example for any other team members with texting inclinations.

After the meeting, Holly stopped by Emily's office to see if she wanted to go to lunch. Her face was beet red. "What's the matter with you?" Holly asked.

Emily was a little embarrassed. "Brett and I have just been at odds about how we're interpreting a business requirement," Emily responded.

Holly knew Brett tended to have strong opinions. He also didn't like people disagreeing with him. Holly had had her share of disagreements with him and immediately empathized with Emily. "Wanna talk about it over lunch?"

"Not really, but the lunch part sounds good," said Emily with the hint of a smile.

The clank of silverware and trays filled the company cafeteria. Holly and Emily meandered throughout the area trying to decide what looked good. Their office building provided a full cafeteria with many of the company's food items prepared in various ways. The food was good and it was subsidized by the company, so the price was always right.

"So, tell me about this difference with Brett," Holly said after they settled in at a table.

Emily rolled her eyes indicating that she wanted to forget about it. "It's really nothing. He wanted to change some of the business requirements to make it work for his design. I pushed back at him but he wouldn't listen to me. Now I have to go back to the business people to see if they'll give in on some of their requirements to fit the design."

"That sounds ass-backwards to me," Holly said. "Why would we change business requirements to fit our design? We should design it to fit their requirements."

"Yes, but they may be willing to give in on these requirements. And I didn't want to get into it with him. You know how obstinate he can be sometimes," Emily said.

"Yes, I do," replied Holly. "But I really don't like that approach. Let's talk about the details when we get back upstairs."

Through the rest of the lunch, they put work aside and talked about more enjoyable topics.

When there was a lull in the conversation Emily asked, "So do you like being a project manager?"

"Yes," Holly answered. "I love it."

"I've been thinking about making a career change and was considering project management," Emily said.

Holly's brown eyes brightened up. "You'd be a great project manager Emily. You're very detail oriented."

"I don't know if I'd like it. I mean, I enjoy being a BA. I just thought a change would be good. But managing a project seems like it's just a series of checklists and making sure you check things off."

Holly smiled. "I know a few project managers that manage by checklist. It's an easy mode to get into, especially if you manage similar projects all the time. Most of the project plan is completed for you and you just follow your templates."

"Is that how you manage projects?" asked Emily.

"No," answered Holly. "I mean, I've got my share of checklists and templates. Everyone does. But that's not a replacement for thinking. When we attend our daily stand-up meetings, we go around the room and everybody gives their update. I could just let them go around the room and be done. But I need know what each of their updates means to the status of the project."

"You do ask some pretty good questions. Like this morning when you asked Grant about finishing his task today. You really pushed him to the wall to answer why it wasn't done."

"You can't just go through the motions," Holly said. "Checklists help you remember a lot of things, but you can't just go into 'robot checklist mode,' where all you do is follow a predefined list of activities and tasks. For one thing, there's not a lot of challenge to that. But the big thing is, for a project with any complexity, you'll probably fail. For each checklist item you have to stop and ask yourself, 'Why am I doing this?' There's more to it than doing the bare minimum to cross it off the list."

"Thanks, Holly," said Emily. "I may just be Harrison-Lee's next project manager."

When they got back from lunch, Holly sat down with Emily for a more formal discussion. "Before we think about going to the business people, I want to understand more about the design and why Brett wants to do this."

Emily showed Holly the section of the business requirements in question. It dealt with an electronic comparison that was supposed to take place between an invoice file and a payment file. "I think the invoice file should be used as the base file to be compared to the payment file. Brett thinks we should use the payment file."

"What's the difference?" Holly asked.

"There's a many to many relationship between the two files. You can get different outcomes depending on which file you used as the basis," Emily responded.

"I'm going to schedule a meeting with you and Brett to make sure I understand both arguments," Holly said.

The following morning, Holly sat down with Brett and Emily in her office. "Brett, I understand we're considering going to the business team and asking them to make some requirements changes in order to avoid making some design changes. Is that true?" she began.

"If we do it Emily's way," Brett replied, "I would have to make some changes to the database design."

Holly had Brett walk her through the differences between the two approaches and tried to drill down on how it would impact them. "How much time would it take to make the changes that would allow this functionality?" she finally asked.

"At least a week, maybe more." Brett replied.

"How much more?" she countered.

"I don't know," answered Brett. "I'd have to go back and study it some more."

"I'm not going to go back to the business team and ask them to change their requirements unless I can tell them how it will impact the project," Holly said. "I need you to either keep this design or tell me more accurately what the changes will cost the project. When will you know that?"

Brett didn't answer at first. He was trying to manage his irritation. He wasn't used to people pushing back at him like that. "I've got some documents at my desk that will help me get some specific impact information to you."

"Great," said Holly. "I'll go with you and we can figure it out together."

Brett's shoulders fell slightly, but he said nothing to object.

After spending just a few minutes at Brett's desk, Holly wondered if strangulation of a developer could be justified. She sat across him wondering if he even noticed her brown eyes burning holes through him. Meanwhile, he perused through his My Documents folder, looking for the latest copy of his design specification.

Finally, she couldn't hold her tongue any longer. "Do you keep every file in your My Documents folder?"

"Yeah, why?"

"Why? Because you're going through hundreds of documents trying to find it. Why don't you create subdirectories for the different projects you work on and then other subdirectories within them for different categories of documents?"

Brett shook his head. "Then I just end up digging through all the different layers of folders. I'll spend more time navigating through a folder structure than it takes to find the document my way."

"That's just not true," said Holly. "There is some overhead involved with organizing things and keeping them organized, but it's much faster and more efficient to be organized."

"I just don't think so," argued Brett.

"Let's test it," Holly said. "Do me a favor and give it a try for two weeks. Set up a directory structure and see if it's easier to find things. If you don't like it after two weeks, you can go back to your old way."

Brett wasn't convinced, but he was tired of Holly's complaining. This wasn't his first time hearing it. "Okay, I'll give it two weeks."

Holly spent the next thirty minutes helping Brett set up directories for each project. They set up directories for miscellaneous documents like coding standards and articles he wanted to read. Then, within each project directory, they created subdirectories for categories such as Technical Documentation, Business Requirements, and Correspondence.

After all of the directory structures were created, they filed away all of the folders that Brett had heaped together in the My Documents folder. She explained to him that whenever he created a new document or received one in an e-mail, that he should file it in the appropriate folder. "It only takes a couple of seconds to navigate the directory structure to file it away versus all the time you spend looking for it," she said.

Brett was not completely convinced, but agreed to give it a try, if for no other reason than to prove her wrong. "I'll give it a try," he said, "and then we'll talk in two weeks."

"Deal," Holly said, smiling for the first time in about an hour. Then she continued, "now, let's take a look at this change."

Brett showed her the design documents that he and his team had pulled out for their analysis. He walked her through the change and how it would affect their design. As he went through it, he realized that their current database design may be able to handle the design either way.

"That's great," Holly said, trying not to sound condescending. "So there are no design changes necessary?"

Brett shook his head slowly. "Not at this time," he said without making eye contact.

"Thank you, Brett, for figuring out a way to make this work. I really appreciate it."

"You're welcome," Brett replied a bit sheepishly.

Back at her desk, Holly sat down and began to run her daily bug summary. Analyzing the trends over the past week, she noticed that the number of open defects indicated that the team was falling behind in fixing bugs. With only a short time left in this iteration, she wanted to have most of them closed before moving on.

She began thinking about what could make the team more productive without adding time to their work week. Holly knew that each developer commuted an average of about an hour each way to work per day. Her preference was to have everyone on the team located on site. She believed that it increased productivity to work in a team room environment to facilitate immediate communication and promote teamwork. There was also the fifteen-minute daily stand-up meeting. That always worked best when everyone was on-site.

As she tumbled it around in her head, she began thinking of a compromise solution option. What if she allowed each developer to work from home one day per week? If each team member agreed to use the saved commute time to fix defects, it would give each developer two additional hours of productivity each week on average. Spreading that across her eight developers would give the team sixteen hours of additional productivity each week.

Based on her tracking statistics, Holly knew that the average bug fix took each developer about forty minutes to investigate and fix. Some took a few hours but many simple ones are resolved in much less time. This would allow them to fix more than twenty additional bugs per week.

She analyzed how the team processed the defects to see if there were improvements in that process to increase productivity. As part of her analysis, she noted that when a new defect was created, it was assigned to the person that wrote that module of code. However, if the bug was deemed to be a data issue, the developer would assign it to someone on the database team.

The quality assurance tester usually knew when a defect was a data issue. Holly decided that the QA tester should try to make the initial bug assignment to the rightful owner. She believed this would reduce the time spent by the programmer going through bugs that are not his or her responsibility.

Holly found that by being a little creative in identifying ways to improve productivity, she didn't need to resort to making the team work more hours.

With another problem solved, Holly decided to call it a day.

The corridor along the offices and cubicles was long and empty. Holly walked along the vacant line of empty seats and cluttered desks. She checked her phone; it was seven o'clock. Well, at least it's earlier than last night, she thought. She still had about an hour's worth of documents to review at home.

The next morning as Holly prepared to start her day, Sam stopped by her office. "Got a minute?" he asked.

"Sure," she answered. "What's up?"

"I was going through the time reports and saw that you had sixty-five hours last week. How many hours do you have so far this week?"

"I'm not sure," Holly said, "but I know I'm already close to forty."

"I'm a little concerned about you burning out," said Sam. "There are going to be tough weeks where you work long hours, but your performance is going to be affected if you do it on a regular basis."

Holly gave a half-shrug and said, "There's just a lot to do lately. I don't want the project to get behind."

"What kind of activities are you doing on a daily basis that requires so much time?" Sam asked.

"A lot of the day is taken up by meetings. I don't get around to reviewing the business requirements documents and technical designs until all the meetings are done. I usually end up leaving around seven."

"Do you have to be in every one of those meetings?"

"I probably don't have to, but I want to make sure I'm in the know as they define the business requirements."

"Holly, I don't want to tell you how to do your job," said Sam, "but I want to give you some advice that I learned early in my management career. I was a lot like you. I wanted to go to every meeting so I could know what's going on. But there's not enough time in the day. I taught my staff how to write good meeting minutes and to distribute them within a day of the meeting."

"We do that now," Holly said.

"Then why do you have to be in every meeting?" asked Sam. "Have them provide the meeting minutes and keep you in the loop. You also have the daily stand up. They're supposed to keep you updated in that meeting on any decisions made in their meetings from the previous day, right?"

"I suppose," said Holly, not fully convinced.

"Did you say you were reviewing technical designs?"

"Yes," said Holly wincing slightly, realizing that it wasn't necessary for the project manager to review technical designs.

"The hardest part I found about being a manager was that I was less of a doer," said Sam. "I wasn't involved in the details as much anymore. It took me a while to let the details go and let my team handle them. You've got to let your team do their job. And part of their job is to inform you of any issues where they need your input."

"Thanks, Sam" said Holly. "I know you're right. I just need to develop enough of a comfort level to let go of the details."

After Sam left her office, she reviewed her to-do list for the day. She had six meetings scheduled and four documents to review. After going through each task, she e-mailed the coordinators of three of the meetings to let them know she wouldn't be attending, but would be watching for the meeting minutes.

She then e-mailed Kyle to tell him she had not reviewed the technical design document he sent to her, but would defer to his judgment on all technical design decisions.

That afternoon at four-thirty, with all of her to-do list items scratched off, she walked out of the office and was greeted by a strange sight: daylight.

Lessons Learned

Tip #84 – Mediate conflicts when necessary

Some people avoid confrontation because they are uncomfortable with personal conflict. Others avoid it because they don't know how to confront it. Whenever there is a difference of opinion within the project where two parties appear to be at a stalemate, it is the project manager's responsibility to bring the parties together to facilitate a solution. Although this may be uncomfortable for all involved at the beginning, in most cases, everyone involved walks away satisfied with the outcome and surprised at how simple the resolution turned out to be.

Tip #85 – Target alignment with the business

In the course of a project, team members may be inclined to seek out easier or faster ways to do something.

Other times, team members may lose sight of the goal and steer the project off course.

When any of these situations occur, the project manager should remind the team of the ultimate goal of aligning all they do with what the business users requested.

When Brett wanted to change the business requirements to better fit his design, Holly made sure that the business requirements were given priority.

Tip #86 – Get organized and help others to get organized

An organized project manager is able to prioritize responsibilities, resulting in better productivity. This includes knowing where documents – in paper form as well as electronic – are located for quick and easy access.

Additionally, the project manager should mentor the members of her team to be organized. Disorganized team members are more likely to be inefficient, causing missed deadlines and delays for other project team members. This affects the project as a whole.

Tip #87 – Stop bad behavior early

When Holly saw Dominic and Eric texting each other in the requirements meeting, she knew that she needed to deal with it promptly. The longer team members are allowed to get away with any type of disruptive behavior, a precedence is set that could cause other team members to believe it is acceptable behavior.

Tip #88 – Be an independent thinker

Organized project managers generally live by their to-do lists. Checklists are a great assistance to most busy people to help them keep track of tasks and priorities.

But a good project management knows that the checklist is just a tool that doesn't keep her from stopping to think about everything she does. Having an adaptable approach will help a project manager keep the correct focus and ensure that the right priorities are being followed.

Tip #89 – Be creative

When a project falls behind, the normal reaction by a project manager is to ask – or require – the team to work longer days and weekends to get caught up. But working more hours doesn't always translate to more productivity by the team. It can hurt morale and cause team members to burn out quicker, resulting in lower productivity than if the team had just worked a normal forty-hour week.

Another common approach is to add people to the team. Late into a project, that approach is less likely to translate to higher productivity. When managers throw additional bodies to a failing project, the existing team spends more time training the new team members, further reducing productivity.

Instead of implementing inefficient solutions such as increasing hours or adding team members to increase productivity, Holly dug a little deeper and made some observations which led her to some more creative solutions that improved the team's productivity without adding the burden of more work hours on them.

Tip #90 – Learn how to delegate

Most projects have so many details that it's hard for a project manager to resist getting involved. It can be difficult determining which details are necessary to be involved in and which ones are unnecessary.

It is important for a project manager to allow the team members to handle detailed information, attend the necessary meetings and report issues and risks to them. This allows the project manager to focus on the important decisions of the project and to avoid burning out before the project ends.

Chapter 23 – Difficult Decisions

Chad was watching a baseball game on TV as Holly tapped away at her laptop.

"How much work do you have?" he asked.

"Maybe ten more minutes," she responded. "I've got a meeting Friday that I'm preparing for."

"Is this a big meeting?" he asked.

"There are a few high-level executives," she said. "I'm preparing the agenda and want to make sure I've worded the purpose well and have all of the discussion items we need to talk about. I want to send it out tomorrow morning so all of the attendees have at least a day to review and know what to expect."

"The bigger the meeting, the more important it is," Chad said. "I wish more people I worked with spent a few minutes of planning like that. Our meetings would go a lot smoother."

The next morning while Holly worked at her desk, Emily stuck her head in and said. "I thought you hated meetings."

"I do, why?"

"Well, you scheduled a meeting for this afternoon to prepare for a meeting we're having tomorrow," said Emily. "That just seems like a lot of meetings."

Holly put up her hands in a surrender mode. "The only thing I hate more than meetings is badly run meetings. If you, Paul, and I get together for a half hour today, that's an hour and a half total time. With ten people in tomorrow's meeting, I think a pre-planning meeting is worth it."

"I hadn't looked at it like that," said Emily.

"Besides that," continued Holly, "there are some high-level people in tomorrow's meeting. Their time is valuable. If we show them we're organized and run an efficient meeting, that's always a good reflection on us."

Later that afternoon in the pre-meeting, Emily discussed the requirements that she would review in the next day's meeting. Holly was particularly concerned about a set of the requirements where Emily did not have a full set of documentation. The business rules for storage and retrieval of frozen foods at Harrison Distribution Systems had never been documented in one single set of documentation. Some of it had been documented in a warehousing application they had purchased. The rest of it was documented within two other applications that were written internally about ten years ago. "How did you handle the business rules for the frozen foods?" Holly asked.

"We didn't have time to document those rules. We actually just referred to the other applications for the business rules for that area," Emily responded.

"Don't you think that will be problematic with Matt, the QA manager?" Holly asked. "They'll have to write test scripts for that and they might have some trouble if there are no business requirements defined for them."

"They're defined, just not within our system," Emily defended.

"Well, they're not well defined," said Holly. "And they're scattered across at least three different systems."

"Just between you and me," Emily said, "I'm hoping Matt doesn't realize the requirements are missing. I'll probably just go over that section fairly quickly. With any luck, we'll get everyone's approval without that section of the requirements."

"What if he does catch it?" asked Holly. "Won't that set you back a week or so to document it if he holds out?"

"Yes," said Emily, "that's why we're trying to avoid it."

Holly thought about it for a few seconds and finally said, "I don't agree with trying to put it past them."

"We're not trying to sneak something past them," said Emily. "The documentation exists, we just don't want to rewrite it in our documentation."

"I think I'd like to talk to Matt first and see what he thinks," Holly said.

As Holly started to close the meeting, Emily said, "One other thing, Holly. I was talking to Chris and John, my BAs. They have a couple of issues. Chris is working on the data conversion requirements. He told me he was behind schedule by two days and John is writing requirements for the canned beverage segment. He's behind by five days. I've been focused on John's five-day delay.

Looking at the overall plan, Holly saw that the data conversion was actually on the critical path.

"What are you doing about Chris's delay?" Holly asked.

"It's only a two-day delay, so I'm not too worried about it," replied Emily.

Holly pointed out that even though the delay was shorter, that it was more significant.

Emily resisted. "It seems to me that the five-day delay would be more important to reduce."

Holly pointed out the dependencies and explained how Chris's two-day delay could delay the project more than John's five-day delay.

Although Emily understood, she thought it was counter-intuitive. "I just thought you'd address the biggest delay first," she said.

"Not always," said Holly. "You look at the effect each delay will have on the project, not the size of the individual delay. We have the option of bringing in some additional BAs on a contractual basis. If we brought in two or three new people, do you think they would be able to help us catch up?"

"Well, it depends," Emily responded. "Do they know the food manufacturing industry? Have they had experience using the technologies we're using? If they have deep experience in both of those, we could bring them up to speed within a few weeks. We'd continue to be behind during that period, but we'd eventually catch up."

Holly looked at the staffing plan and saw that some other business analysts were not being fully utilized. "We have some BAs sitting, waiting for some tasks in the critical path to complete before they start their work. Can we get them started earlier? Why do they have to wait for the previous tasks to finish?"

"They could probably start earlier," said Emily. "They were set up as dependencies to be involved in the business requirements review, but since we're in a bind, that's kind of a luxury. We could have them start each of their tasks as much as a week earlier."

On her way back to her desk, Holly stopped by Matt's office and spoke to him about the frozen foods documentation. She asked him if referring to the other systems would be acceptable to him.

"We've done that before with other applications and it's turned out to be a lot of extra work," Matt said. "I'd rather we document it here."

"Will you approve the requirements without that section in it?" Holly asked Matt.

"I don't want to delay the project," Matt answered, "but it will set our team back, not having those requirements in there. We'll have to go back to all of those applications and review requirements from each of them to determine how to test the new system."

"I have an idea," Holly said. "What if I work with one of the BAs to pull them together from the different areas they're currently located? In tomorrow's session, we'll review everything except the frozen foods requirements. You can approve everything except that section. Once we get the frozen foods document completed, we'll review that with you separately. That way, we can get your approval and start work on development without any delays."

"That works for me," Matt said with a smile.

Holly left Matt's office satisfied that she had figured out a solution with him. She was glad that she was proactive enough to talk to him without trying to get his approval and avoiding a discussion about a large set of missing documentation.

The next day, the meeting went down without a hitch. The agenda that Holly developed allowed them to drive through the necessary discussion points. Knowing what they would cover and knowing each person's role for each topic allowed them to end the meeting fifteen minutes earlier than planned.

As Sam walked out of the meeting, he turned to the three of them and said, "Nicely run meeting. Thanks for the extra fifteen minutes."

Back at her desk, an e-mail immediately raised Holly's eyebrows. With the subject line that read "Application on new platform," it piqued Holly's interest enough to open it before the others in her queue. The first sentence made her heart beat just a little bit faster. When she finished reading it for the second time, she sat back in her chair in a defeated gesture, thinking, who needs coffee when you get e-mails like this?

She pulled up her project plan. With it still displayed on her tablet screen, she carried it over to Kyle's office and wrapped her knuckles on his door.

"Got a minute?" she asked.

"Yes, I do," he said as he turned away from his computer screen.

"I saw your e-mail about moving the application to a new platform," said Holly. "Can you tell me what was behind that decision?"

"Sure," said Kyle. "We were talking yesterday with the architecture team. They had some concerns about the fact that we were writing this application on the X7 platform, which is fairly dated. All of the newer applications are written on the X9 platform, which is more up to date. If we continue on as we're going, we'll just have to do a bunch of rework later this year to move it onto the new platform. We'll save a lot of time doing it now."

"This will extend our project timeline by quite a bit," said Holly.

"It should only extend it a month or so," said Kyle. "If we wait and do it later, there will be a lot more overhead involved. It would probably take at least three months to do it as a separate project."

"I realize that," Holly said with a reproachful impatience in her voice. "We discussed the different platforms at the beginning of the project. We're under a lot of pressure just to have a working, consolidated system ready by July. We met with the Architecture team and representatives from the business and made decisions to cut some things out in order to make that date."

"I wasn't aware of that," Kyle said with a confused look.

"We knew it would be more efficient to do the platform as part of this project, but decided it was worth the extra cost to do it later in order to have the system working when the merger was final," said Holly.

Kyle didn't know what to say.

"In addition," continued Holly, "I've got a team allocated to this project through July, with a few people going beyond that for production support. We can't just extend the project by a month without considering all of the constraints."

"What do you mean by constraints?" asked Kyle.

"Kyle, with a project like this, we're given a budget that covers the contracts with our consultants, the office space we use, and the internal staffing assigned to it. It would be great to include as much functionality and scope as we can to make this the ultimate project. Are you familiar with the triple constraint?"

Kyle shook his head. "No," he said.

Holly got up and walked to the whiteboard in Kyle's office and drew her best effort of a three-legged stool. Above it, she wrote the title *The Triple Constraint*.

"Whenever we have a request for new functionality," Holly said, "we need to address the triple constraint for the project."

In the diagram she labeled each leg. The first leg was labeled *Time*. "The first constraint is time," she said, turning back to Kyle. "This is the finite amount of time available to complete the project. Our project deadline is June thirtieth and that is set in stone based on when the merger will be complete."

Kyle nodded in agreement.

"The second constraint is cost," she explained, labeling the second leg. "This represents how much money has been budgeted to spend on the project. Finally, there is scope," she said, labeling the third leg. "This represents how much functionality and at what level of quality we can include in the project. We can't change one of these constraints without affecting the other two."

Kyle continued to nod as Holly noticed him taking a keen interest. "I didn't realize there was so much involved in the planning of resources. I just thought it would be a good idea to make the platform change and save time in the long run."

"And that makes perfect sense," Holly replied feeling a little less intense. "As long as we have the patient open for surgery, we might as well operate on everything we can. But we have to consider what we're constrained by and live within those parameters."

Holly left Kyle a little frustrated but understanding a little more of the issues she dealt with as a project manager. As she headed back to her office she saw Sam in the hallway. He turned to her and asked, "Do you have a minute?"

"Sure," she said.

He directed her to his office and closed the door. He grabbed a chair at the small table off to the side of the office and indicated for her to sit across from him. He had a grave look on his face that made Holly certain that if Sam looked closely, he could see her heart beating in her chest.

Sam looked her straight in the eye and said, "Pete was let go from the company this morning."

Holly's face showed shock and disbelief. "Really?"

"Yes. I can't reveal too many details, but I had been dealing with him and some issues for quite a while. He had been on a performance improvement plan and I was meeting with him on a regular basis to coach him on some things. One of those things was his attitude. He had a certain cockiness in the way he dealt with his peers."

"You're kidding," Holly said in feigned disbelief.

Sam showed a slight smile and continued. "When you told me about what he said to you the other day, along with some other performance issues, I realized that he wasn't making the progress I was hoping for. I'm sorry if he caused you undue distress for your job."

A thousand thoughts were going through Holly's mind. "A lot of things are starting to fall together. I appreciate you setting my mind at ease the other day and I appreciate you telling me personally today. I really didn't care for Pete so I won't pretend that I'm sorry he's gone. I'm just glad it's over. I'm sure you are, too."

Sam smiled and nodded. "It's never a pleasant experience, but it's part of the job."

Holly left Sam's office with mixed emotions. She didn't like to hear about anyone losing their job. But she was pretty excited to share her newfound information with Chad.

Lessons Learned

Tip #91 – Make meetings productive

Spending time to make sure her agenda was complete and accurate for the meeting attendees allowed Holly to set the appropriate expectations for her meeting. If anyone were to go off-topic during the meeting, she could refer back to the agenda to bring the meeting back on track.

Additionally, the agenda provided everyone involved with the objective of meeting and the list of everyone invited to the meeting.

Tip #92 - Plan time for pre-meeting meetings if necessary

When a meeting with a large number of attendees or with high-level executives is being planned, it can be beneficial to hold a pre-meeting to plan what each presenter will present, the order people will present, what the team wants to say – and in some cases – what the team doesn't want to say.

Holding a short planning meeting can make the difference between a well-run meeting and a disastrous one.

Tip #93 – Be proactive

Instead of hoping that Matt did not notice missing requirements, Holly was proactive in telling him about it in advance and worked out an agreement with him. This allowed her team and Matt's team to be more efficient.

It also avoided the situation of having to be reactive if Matt noticed the missing requirements during the meeting.

Tip #94 – Determine the impact of issues and delays

A good project manager anticipates the effect that an issue or delay will have on the project. Some issues look worse than others when compared side-by-side.

Comparing their effect on the project helps the project manager to set priorities and make the right decisions. When Emily presented Holly with two delays, she assumed the longer delay would be the greater impact. Holly determined that the shorter delay ultimately would have a greater impact on the project.

Tip #95 - Keep your eye on the critical path

The most important sequence of tasks in a project is the critical path. This is the longest set of contiguous tasks in the plan. There may be more than one in a project. Any delay of a task on the critical path will result in a project delay. A project manager must focus on the tasks in this path to make sure that the project is not delayed.

Holly recognized that the shorter task identified by Emily was actually part of the critical path. The longer task was not part of this sequence and its delay was less likely to have a significant effect on the project.

As a result, while she focused her attentions on completing all tasks, she focused more attention on the critical path tasks to make sure that they were completed in a timely manner.

Tip #96 – Know when to crash and when to fast track the project

Crashing the schedule means adding new people to the project to get things done faster. But just as nine women can't have a baby in one month, it's not always possible to get things done faster with more people. Often, adding people causes bigger delays. Significant analysis should be performed before adding such an expense to insure that this will actually increase a team's velocity.

Fast tracking a schedule means performing tasks in parallel to reduce the critical path. Great care should be taken with this approach as well. Dependencies are established for a reason. Starting a dependent task before the previous task is completed could result in mistakes that cause rework which can result in even longer delays.

Tip #97 –Manage the triple constraint

Every project manager should become familiar with the competing constraints of time, cost, and scope. Each component is limited on any project. If one is increased, the other two will most likely be affected.

Once Kyle understood the constraints Holly was trying to balance, he was able to understand why moving to the new platform should not be added to the scope of the project.

Chapter 24 – Final Stages

The tables had no white tablecloths and the décor in the restaurant was at least ten to fifteen years old. Holly knew they weren't in the fanciest restaurant in town. She didn't have enough budget for fancy. She did know that everyone at the table was smiling and having a good time.

It was July second. The team had worked hard and they had just taken the project live on time and within budget. After all of the hard work and long hours, Holly felt it was important to celebrate and recognize the team's efforts.

After the waiter took everyone's orders, Holly stood up and clinked her glass with her fork.

"Is somebody supposed to kiss?" Brett asked.

Holly smiled shaking her head. "I just want to take a moment to thank all of you for your hard work. This was a busy several months for us and everyone pitched in and got it done. The developers showed their commitment to not only getting things done on time, but it was quality work. The quality assurance testers did a great job identifying issues and the business analysts worked with both teams to translate what the business wanted to everyone. So here's a toast to each of you for your efforts. Thank you."

Everybody raised their glass and basked in their team glory.

And then Holly added, "Now Brett, you can kiss Grant if you'd like."

Everyone laughed.

The next day, Emily stopped to thank Holly for the team celebration. "What are you working on?" she asked.

"Just a few project close-down items," Holly replied. "Speaking of that, are you coming to the lessons-learned session on Friday?"

"I saw your invite for that, what is that for?" Emily asked.

"After the project has gone live we meet with all of the project's stakeholders to talk about what we would like to see improved on future projects," said Holly.

"That doesn't sound so pleasant," said Emily. "Do you expect a lot of finger pointing?"

"No, I don't allow that," said Holly. "I keep it very positive. We want to see how we can improve. We also talk about what worked well and add that to the list so that we make sure to continue doing things right too."

"Well, I've been keeping an eye on things since we went live," said Emily. "Most of the feedback is from people inquiring how to do things, but the system has stayed up consistently and has been working fine. I think it's been a great success."

"I agree," said Holly. "I think the entire project was a big success. But there's always either room for improvement or things that improved our performance that we want to make sure we continue to do on future projects."

"It might just be an interesting meeting after all," Emily said.

That Friday, after the team had met for over an hour, the document Holly had projected on the screen listed fifteen lessons learned and nine items the project team thought worked so well that they wanted to document it for future projects.

As the team members filed out, Emily stuck around to walk Holly back to her desk. "That went well. I was surprised how positive it was," Emily said.

"It's supposed to be positive," said Holly. "It's what constructive criticism is all about. Lessons learned isn't about saying 'Emily, you screwed up.' It's about saying this happened and here's what we should do to avoid having it happen again."

"What do you do with the list?"

"I'll send it out to the team and store it in the repository with other lists that have been compiled for other projects," said Holly. "When a project manager starts a new project they're supposed to check the list."

"So what's next?" Emily asked. "What are you going to do now?"

"What do you mean?"

"Do you start a new project this week or will they give you a break for a while?" asked Emily.

"I'll still be on this project for another couple of weeks," Holly explained. "There's still a lot to do."

"Like what?"

"The project needs to be closed down." Holly held up the Project Close-Down checklist on her desk. "I need to submit performance evaluations for every team member, make sure the latest version of every document is stored in the repository, and decommission all of the test servers back to the infrastructure team. I may actually be working on this project part time for another couple of months just tying up loose ends."

"I had no idea there were so many additional things to do," said Emily.

"That's because a lot of project managers don't do them," said Holly. "Once the project goes live they move on to their next project and none of the housekeeping gets done. It makes it hard for the people working on the next phase or who want to refer to documentation that wasn't archived appropriately. It's actually a full phase in our software development life cycle."

227

"So, no other big celebrations?" Emily asked, a little disappointed.

"Chad's taking me out to dinner tonight. That's my celebration," Holly said with satisfaction.

Holly got out of Chad's car and stepped onto the parking lot. Chad was taking her to her favorite restaurant, La Dolce Vita.

The hostess greeted them with a wide smile. She recognized them as regulars. She led them through the restaurant to the patio area. The tables on the patio were shaded by an awning.

They enjoyed fresh Italian bread with olive oil and grated Parmesan cheese. When their wine came, they toasted to the end of the Merge-Tech project.

"I haven't seen you this relaxed in months, Holly," Chad said.

"It's a huge relief to have this project completed," she said.

"For both of us," he said as he held up his wine glass one more time.

They enjoyed a wonderful meal and conversation. After the waiter cleared their plates, they contemplated dessert. The contemplation was purely academic. They always shared the tiramisu.

After they placed the dessert order, Holly saw the violin player heading in their direction. "Look, I think he's going to play for us," she said. He stopped at their table and she recognized the song he was playing. "Chad, that's the first song we ever danced to."

When she turned to look at him, she saw that he wasn't in his seat. She thought he had dropped something. He was down on his knee. Then she saw the small open box with a beautiful diamond in it.

When her brown eyes made contact with his, he began. "Holly, I love you. I want to spend the rest of my life with you. Would you make me the happiest man in the world and marry me?"

Holly was in shock. After a moment's pause, tears came to her eyes as she blurted out, "Of course!"

Every table on the patio began to applaud. She stood up and gave Chad a hug. He put the ring on her finger and the full restaurant's applause erupted again as she held it up for all to see.

The tiramisu arrived and they took their seats. While they savored their dessert, an occasional couple leaving the restaurant stopped by to congratulate them.

Chad turned to Holly and said, "I'm glad to see you so happy."

"Happy doesn't even begin to describe it. Not only am I marrying the man of my dreams, this wedding is going to be the best project I've ever managed."

Lessons Learned

Tip #98 –Celebrate successes

Project teams put in long hours and a lot of dedicated work. It is important for a project manager to recognize that and reward the team with occasional celebrations. Celebrations don't need to be fancy and expensive. In fact, it is better to spend less on the celebrations but have them more frequently.

During these celebrations, the project manager should take a brief moment to say thank you and point out the major accomplishments of the team.

Tip #99 – Record lessons learned

Every project has situations and occurrences that could be improved. It is important, once the project is complete, to do a review with the full team to discuss areas for improvement for future projects. The team should also discuss things that went well so they can repeat those practices in future projects.

It is critical to maintain a positive approach to this. When errors and any area for improvement are discussed, finger pointing and blame should not take place. The focus should be on how it can be done better in the future.

Tip #100 – Formally close the project

After the project has been delivered, there are still close-down items that should be performed by the project manager. There is often a tendency to move on or to put the project in the past once the main functionality has been delivered. But important tasks must still be performed.

The project manager should close down the project by storing all related documentation in a permanent repository, decommission any servers no longer needed, and perform performance reviews for any project team members.

Tip #101 – Always be ready for the next project

If it has been a particularly difficult or long project, it may be beneficial to take some time to relax and recharge one's batteries. At some point, the project manager needs to begin thinking about the next challenge. There should always be another project on the horizon.

Thanks for reading Project Management 101. I would really appreciate you leaving a review at the site from which you purchased this book.

Order Lew's other books today:

Consulting 101: 101 Tips for Success in Consulting

The Reluctant Mentor: How Baby Boomers and Millenials Can Mentor Each Other in the Modern Workplace

Glossary – 101 Project Management Terms

Agile: A project methodology that advocates flexibility through iterative processes. After each iteration, results are shared with the business users to determine priorities for the next iteration. The opposite methodology is waterfall.

Assumption: A statement which the project team considers to be true in order to move forward on the project. Assumptions are stated to the business users for their agreement and acceptance, usually at the beginning of the project.

BA: See *Business analyst*

Backlog: See *Project backlog*

Baseline: An initial project plan that has been formally established. New updates to the plan will require re-baselining.

BRD: See *Business Requirements Document*

Bug: In software development, functionality that is inconsistent with the business requirements.

Business Analyst (BA): Role in software development that performs analysis and definition of business requirements. A liaison between business and technical teams.

Business Requirements: Details explaining how functionality in software should work as specified by the business users.

Business Requirements Document (BRD): A high-level summary of business requirements as specified by business users. The purpose of this document is to explain to software developers how a software system shall perform business functionality

Change Control: A formal project management process in which changes to the original scope are identified, documented, approved and added to a project plan.

Change Log: A document which tracks all requested changes to the scope of a project, noting potential impact, whether it has been approved and, if approved, how it is added to the project plan.

Change Request: A document which details a requested change to the scope of a project and the impact the change will have upon the project if approved. A change request is submitted to the business user team for approval.

Communications Plan: A document which formally defines major communication flows within a project. Recurring meetings are described including frequency, attendees, days and times, and purpose of each meeting.

Constraint: A limiting aspect of a project that must be managed. Project managers often discuss the triple constraint, in which they must balance the time, cost, and scope of a project.

Contingency: When estimating work effort, an additional time added to the estimate to cover unknowns.

Cost Variance: When cost to a project is below or above the amount originally planned.

Crashing: A project management process in which resources are added to a project in an effort to reduce the duration. Additional risk is introduced because, while it usually involves additional cost, increased productivity is not always guaranteed.

Critical Path: The sequence of dependent tasks in a project plan that represent the longest duration within the project or phase. Any delays in a critical path task will result in delaying the project timeline. There may be multiple critical paths in a project.

Daily Scrum: See *Stand-up meeting*

Defect: See *Bug*

Deliverable: Any output product generated on a project.

Demo: A demonstration of the product performed, usually for a user group, to show functionality created to-date.

Dependency: A task on a project that must be performed prior to performance of another task.

Done, Done, Done: Common terminology in Agile software development to indicate that a task is not complete until all follow up steps have taken place, including communicating status to dependent downstream team members.

Duration: Estimating aspect which takes into account the number of hours or days a task will take including any lag time or lead time.

Estimating: A high-level approximation assigned to each project task to provide an idea of the cost and/or duration of time the task will take to perform.

Fast-Tracking: A project management process in which tasks that were originally scheduled to be performed in sequence are performed in parallel to decrease the duration of the project. Additional risk is introduced because additional rework can result if one of the parallel tasks creates issues for the other.

Finish-To-Finish Dependency: A dependency when multiple tasks are scheduled to complete at the same time; usually created when a task is dependent on the completion of multiple tasks.

Finish-To-Start Dependency: A dependency that occurs when a task cannot begin until a preceding task has been completed.

FRD: See *Functional Requirements Document*

Functional Requirements Document (FRD): A requirements document which goes to a deeper level of definition than the Business Requirements Document. While the BRD defines what must be done, the FRD defines how it will be performed.

Gantt Chart: A bar chart which shows task durations and how tasks are related to one another. Tasks are listed on the vertical axis while time is represented horizontally.

Integration Testing: A quality assurance testing approach in which related components are tested together to verify that they exchange data correctly.

Issue: A problem that may or may not impact the project plan. Issues are generally categorized by severity (i.e. Low, Medium, High, Critical), determined based on its impact.

Issues Log: A document in which all project issues - current and closed - are recorded and tracked.

Iteration: In agile project management, a period of time - usually between 3-5 weeks - in which a specified set of work is completed. At the end of an iteration, the project team may present the completed work to the business team in the form of a Demo.

Iterative Project Management: An agile form of project management that directs the team to complete tasks in iterations of 3-5 week periods. Work is planned at the beginning of each iteration with daily meetings for each team member to provide a brief status update.

Kick-off Meeting: A meeting held at the beginning of a project to introduce and explain the objective and scope of the project. Separate kick-off meetings may be held with the internal and external stakeholders.

Lag Time: A delay between two tasks.

Lead Time: A period of time that one task may overlap with another task which is already in progress.

Lean Programming: A software development concept based on lean manufacturing that emphasizes elimination of waste, fast delivery and continuous learning for better efficiencies and higher quality.

Lessons Learned: A project management practice in which the team meets at the end of a project, project phase, or iteration to review areas that can be improved and practices that the team suggests continuing for better efficiency and continuous learning.

Level of Effort: High-level estimate of a task or group of tasks which gives a ballpark range for the amount of work required.

Methodology: A series of pre-defined methods and practices that prescribe so called "best practices" for managing the various phases of a project.

Milestone: Checkpoints at various times within a project which allow management to measure whether the project has met certain objectives.

One-On-One: A private meeting between two people, usually a manager or mentor and an employee, to discuss various topics such as status, career goals, and morale.

Percent Complete: A measurement in which the amount of work completed is estimated to show status. There are areas of the project, such as testing which this measurement can be effective. Areas such as software development are based more on judgment and can be suspect to inaccuracies and even deception.

PMI: See *Project Management Institute*

PMO: See *Project Management Office*

PMP: See *Project Management Professional*

Post-mortem: See *Lessons Learned*

Program: A consolidated set of related projects whose management is coordinated, usually with an overriding program manager.

Project: A finite set of tasks and activities with a defined beginning and end which accomplish a specifically defined outcome.

Project Backlog: A list of business requirements (or stories) in an agile project from which the team selects in order to plan an iteration or sprint.

Project Charter: A document created at the beginning of a project to define the purpose, scope, assumptions and primary stakeholders of the project.

Project Close-Down: Phase of a project in which the project manager performs housekeeping activities to formally close the project.

Project Management: Processes and activities of planning, monitoring, controlling and organizing work for a project.

Project Management Institute: A not-for-profit organization for project managers with the objective of advancing the science of project management.

Project Management Office: Department within a company which develops and enforces standardization, processes and tools with the objective of creating a more consistent and efficient approach to project management throughout the organization.

Project Management Professional: Professional certification provided by the Project Management Institute designed to improve the success rate of projects.

Project Plan: A formal document to provide a detailed list of project tasks. The project plan can be in the form of a Project Backlog in an agile environment, or a detailed plan which provides task assignments, estimates and a schedule for all tasks on a project.

Project Scope: The defined amount of work and features that have been agreed upon by all stakeholders to complete a project.

Project Sponsor: An individual or team that provides the funding and other resources to a project, responsible for obtaining internal commitment to the project and supporting the project manager in successful completion of the project.

QA: See *Quality Assurance*

Quality assurance (QA): The planning process to ensure that software is developed according to business requirements. Testing is performed in multiple iterations according to a formal testing plan to verify that the software is bug free.

RACI Matrix: A matrix that identifies for each major deliverable, the stakeholders that are Responsible, Accountable, Consulted and Informed.

Release: In an agile environment, the resulting product of one or more iterations of work that is delivered to the user community.

Requirements: See *Business Requirements*

Resource Leveling: An activity, usually performed by a project manager, to reassign tasks, extend dates, and make related adjustments to a project plan in order to distribute work as evenly as possible without over-allocating team members beyond standard working hours.

Retrospective: See *Lessons Learned*

Risk: The possibility of an occurrence that, if it occurred, could result in impacting the project. Analysis in performed by a project manager to identify as many risks as possible and identify strategies to deal with their occurrence.

Risk Acceptance: The practice of responding to a risk by not taking any action.

Risk Avoidance: Taking action to remove the threat of a risk to prevent it from occurring.

Risk Mitigation: Taking action to reduce the likelihood of a risk occurring or reducing the impact of the risk if it actually occurs.

Risk Register: A formal project document in which all identified risks are detailed with the estimated likelihood, probable impacts, and strategies that will be utilized to either avoid, accept or mitigate them.

Schedule Variance: A measurement of project progress comparing the difference of actual work accomplished to the work that was expected to be complete according to the plan.

Scope: See *Project Scope*

Scope Creep: The term used to describe functionality that is added to a project after the formal scope has been defined. Often small pieces of functionality, which seem insignificant individually add up (creep) to become significant changes with significant impact to a project.

Scrum: Form of agile development consisting of small, interdependent teams working in intense development efforts.

Showcase: See *Demo*

Sprint: See *Iteration*

Stakeholder: Any individual or group that is affected, either directly or indirectly, by a project.

Stand-up Meeting: A daily meeting with all members of the development team in which each person stands up and takes turns reporting status on the following three things: What they accomplished since the last meeting; what they plan to accomplish before the next meeting; any obstacles they are facing that need to be removed.

Start-to-Finish Dependency: A dependency when a task cannot begin until another task has started.

Start-to-Start Dependency: A dependency where two tasks must start together.

Statistical Analysis: The application of statistical methods to report completion and budget status of various aspects of a project. These statistics include Cost Performance Index (CPI), Schedule Performance Index (SPI), Earned Value Performance (EVP).

Status Report: A formal deliverable that communicates the status of the project. It usually is delivered on a regular recurring frequency, such as weekly. Status reports should provide a summary of accomplishments for the reporting period, planned accomplishments for the upcoming period and issues and risk that management should address.

Steering Committee: A senior team within the organization which makes strategic decisions regarding a project including investment, cancelation and changes of course.

The project manager reports high-level status to this team, usually less frequently than is performed for the status reporting team.

System Testing: A quality assurance testing approach in which the full system is tested end-to-end to verify that all functionality processes correctly.

Task: The smallest unit of work that is done as part of a project. A task is usually assigned to an individual team member.

Team Norms: A list of common guidelines and practices that the team agrees to follow and hold each other accountable for following. Most team norms are related to acts of mutual respect.

Timebox: The practice of allocating a fixed period of time in order to perform something. When the predefined period of time is finished, the team will use whatever information they have produced.

Triple Constraint: The three primary constraints that a project manager most often must balance: time, cost and scope. When one of these items is changed, it will most like impact one or both of the remaining constraints.

UAT: See *User Acceptance Testing*

Unit Testing: A quality assurance approach in which a single component is tested in isolation. This level of testing is most often performed by the one who developed the component.

User Acceptance Testing (UAT): A quality assurance approach in which the end users perform testing on the application.

Variance: A difference between actual and planned values, usually related to cost, schedule or budget.

Velocity: A measure of the speed at which work is completed by a development team. Velocity is used to determine how much work can be planned for future iterations.

Vendor: External entity that provides products or services to a project.

Waterfall: A project methodology in which each phase of the project (business requirements definition, analysis, system design, development and testing) is performed in sequence. The opposite approach is agile.

About the Author

Lew Sauder has worked as an IT project manager in consulting and non-consulting environments for nearly twenty years.

Lew has a BS in Applied Computer Science from Illinois State University and an MBA from Northwestern University's Kellogg School of Business. He is a certified Project Management Professional (PMP) with the Project Management Institute.

Other books by Lew Sauder

- *Consulting 101: 101 Tips for Success in Consulting*
- *The Reluctant Mentor: How Baby Boomers and Millenials Can Mentor Each Other in the Modern Workplace.*

Made in the USA
Middletown, DE
18 April 2019